Why You NEED This Book

In this book, I will teach you how to transform your life so well that people will literally ask you for advice.

Imagine, 18 months from now, you are no longer stuck in life. You are free to do what you love at any time. You are healthier, happier, fulfilled and productive.

I stumbled upon the 6 secrets to self-discipline and had my 6th dream come true in less than 4 months.

If you feel stuck in life with no way out, you NEED this book.

11 DREAMS

The 3 a.m. Go-Getter

A funny & inspiring story of
relentless pursuit of dreams

SABRINA Y.C. HE

For my parents,
Ze An He & Hui Zhen Zheng

who love me unconditionally and support me to go after my dreams.
Thank you for being independent and strong, so I can focus on making my
dreams become true on the other side of the world. I love you both and
owe you everything.

For my son,
Benjamin Miller

who is the precious gift from God to me. Follow your heart & dream big!
I believe in you. I love you forever and ever.

VI

ACKNOWLEDGMENTS

Special thanks to the following individuals
who helped me to improve the quality of my writing for this book.

Peggy Harris

Femi Olasupo

Lin Miao

Jennie Preece

Jordan Williamson

Judy Trinkle

CONTENTS

Introduction

Section 1: My Stories & Your Takeaways

Section 2: My Secret Recipe to Self-Discipline

Section 3: Too Good to Miss

Quotations

"If you think you can do a thing or not, you're right either way."
(The Reader's Digest, Volume 51, 1947)
-Henry Ford

"When someone tells me 'no,' it doesn't mean I can't do it, it simply means I can't do it with them."
-Karen E. Quinones Miller

"All successful people men and women are big dreamers. They imagine what their future could be, ideal in every respect, and then they work every day towards their distant vision, that goal or purpose."
(Tracy, 2014)
-Brian Tracy

"Not fulfilling your dreams will be a loss to the world, because the world needs everyone's gift---yours and mine."
-Barbara Sher

"Don't let someone else's opinion of you become your reality."
-Les Brown

"If you don't read the newspaper, you're uninformed. If you read the newspaper, you're misinformed."
-Anonymous[1]

---

[1] This is not Mark Twain's quotation. Retrieved from https://www.realclearpolitics.com/articles/2012/12/10/fake_twain_quotes_and_other_hazards_of_twitter_116376-3.html

INTRODUCTION

Who says self-discipline should be hard and boring? Question that opinion! This book is a game changer. Be prepared to transform your life. It puts you into beast mode to take consistent actions, to work towards your dreams, to achieve your desired lifestyle and to do what you love. You will be obsessed with your new awesome lifestyle!

This is NOT a boring self-help book that tells you what to do. Learning is fun and exciting. Immerse your heart and soul into my real-life story and feel the feelings. You will gain insights, inspiration, strength and easy-to-do action plans to achieve the lifestyle that you have always dreamed of, so buckle up, relax and enjoy the ride while you learn.

The Mission of This Book:

To touch millions of people's lives. To show them the path to achieve their dreams. To inspire you who once had dreams when young, to follow your hearts and pursue your dreams. Together, we can make this world a better place where hearts are filled with joy, fulfillment and vibrant color. This book is written for YOU!

What This Book Is About:

I invite you to submerge into my real-life story. Let me guide you through the steps to live your dreams through self-discipline. In this book, you will get to learn:

- My journey & adventures as I worked to achieve my 6 dreams
- Mistakes that I have made and life lessons that I have learned
- My secret recipe for consistent, pleasant and effective self-discipline
- How to find your dreams
- As a bonus, how to deal with loneliness & feel truly happy on your own

Why I Can Help:

Every morning, I get up at 3:00 a.m. to exercise and work on my dreams. I have had 11 dreams since high school, I am currently working on my dream #7. Let me show you the way to achieve your dreams through self-discipline. It is easier than you think.

As a single mom in a foreign country, there were times that I struggled to survive and I had to rebuilt my life from ground zero. If I can do it, you can do it, too!

Why Do I Care:

You were not born just to make a living, pay bills, raise a family and then die. You have a gift in you and a purpose to your life. You are here to make a difference. I see a lot of people that are miserable with their jobs and lives. When I see the sadness on their face, it hurts my heart! This heartache urged me to write this book. You are the reason why this book exists!

Live your dreams, and never settle for less!

SECTION 1

MY STORIES & YOUR TAKEAWAYS

Self-discipline is the master key to make your dreams happen. It is the path to achieve the lifestyle that you have always dreamed of.

Every January, millions of people set new goals and take actions. After around 2 months, the majority of them get hung up due to lack of self-discipline. Why? Because goals are not must-haves.

When we must have our dreams come true before we die, then self-discipline becomes much easier. Dreams are the reasons. Self-discipline is the path. Dreams coming true are the results.

To make it easier, exciting and enjoyable for you to read this book and learn, let me take you on a trip of time traveling. We are going back in time to where I started. Enjoy the ride!

1
THE AVERAGE KID
ON THE BLOCK

"Life is too short to be little (Disraeli, 1844)."
- Benjamin Disraeli

"Sometimes I can hear my bones straining under the
weight of all the lives I'm not living (Foer, 2005)."
- Jonathan Safran Foer

I was born and raised in China. I was an average kid on the block. I got B's at school and had no special talent or skills. I had no idea what I wanted to do or could do for a living when I grew up. To make things worse, the school did not embrace imagination back then. Most parents guided their kids to learn practical subjects in order to get a well-paying job in the future, in other words, to be realistic. To them, dreams were jokes and would never happen.

I am pretty sure that my imagination was about 75% DEAD when I got to high school. I often struggled to think about what I wanted to do in life. Also, I did not know much about the system of society, occupation, and business. I was amazed at how the world managed to run in harmony every day. I was confused and clueless. To figure out what I wanted to do in the future, I needed to have a better understanding of how the world operated first. For that reason, I visited bookstores often. One day, I stumbled upon a book about imagination and dreams. That was a rare find and I could not believe what I found. I was so excited that I bought the book right away and as soon as I got home, I studied it immediately. For the next 2 weeks behind my bedroom door, I read the book religiously and studied it carefully.

It was a step by step workbook to help me figure out what I wanted to achieve in the future. I took every assignment very seriously. Sometimes, it took me hours to work through a single question. It was a lot of thinking and digging deep into my heart. It was a lot of hard work for sure, but it was worth it. After about 2 weeks, I finally came up with my own list of dreams that I wanted to make happen. It was all about what kind of lifestyle and things that I desired for the future. I was happy with what I came up with on my list.

One of the final assignments was to look for magazine pictures that resemble my dreams, cut them out, post them on a board, and look at them every day. Looking at the pictures would remind me of exactly what I wanted in life down the road. I found some beautiful pictures. However, I did not want people to think that I was crazy, so I hid all the pictures in my bookcase and reviewed them when I was alone. Looking at them made me smile.

One day at school, a classmate mentioned that he wanted to get an MBA degree in the United Kingdom someday. I had no idea what MBA was, so I asked him more questions about it. Because he was known for being very smart, athletic and excellent in many different aspects, I was pretty sure that an MBA degree abroad must be a great thing that he was after. That was how I added one more dream to my list.

At that time, I had 7 dreams altogether. I have added a few more since then. By the time I wrote this book, I had 11 dreams.

What Is in it for you:

I had a friend who had big dreams and wanted to do great things for the society. She could not wait to make them happen, but she did not know how. I offered to help her make plans so she could move towards her dreams. Guess what she said? She was not sure about her dreams anymore, and maybe they were just her ideas. After that day, I have not heard from her for a long time.

Almost everybody has dreams. To most people, dreams are just big ideas, things that they want to do, or the lifestyle that they want to have someday. Those are not dreams. They are wants or something great to have someday. There is no action power in those so-called "dreams". No wonder most people do not have their "dreams" come true. To fire up your action power, you need to first find your dreams. Dreams are the most delicate and precious gifts given to you. They are your must-haves before you die. The question is, how can you find your dreams and be certain that those are your dreams?

There is an exercise in section 3 of this book to help you find your dreams. Most importantly, to help you be sure and certain about your dreams. We are not here to wish, to daydream or brainstorm. We are here to dig into our hearts and souls and to find out who we ultimately desire to become. Somehow deep down in our hearts, we already know who we want to become.

2
THE METEOR SHOWER

"The starting point of all achievement is DESIRE. Keep this constantly in mind. Weak desire brings weak results, just as a small fire makes a small amount of heat (Hill, 1937)."
- Napoleon Hill

After I discovered my dreams, I was very excited. Life seemed really good and I was full of hope. However, having self-doubts is human nature. A few weeks later, I started to have self-doubts. Had anyone around me have their dreams come true before? Even if just one dream had come true, I really NEEDED to hear it. I thought that it would be a great idea to ask my English teacher from school. Afterall, English teachers had more opportunity to be influenced by western culture and education, thus they seemed more open minded. I was sure that she would encourage me to go after my dreams. One day after lunch at school, I ran into my English teacher. She was playing badminton with her husband. I remembered that day vividly. It was a sunny day. Little birds were resting in the trees. I was excited and anxious as I was walking towards her.

Me, "Excuse me, may I ask you a question?"

"Yes, of course."

I asked, "Can dreams come true?"

She paused and thought. I could see that she was looking into her past and trying to come up with her own conclusion.

She sighed, "When I was younger, I had dreams. None of them came true, so I decided to forget about them and move on. I think dreams are not realistic. I have been enjoying my life as it is."

I thanked her and she went back to her game.

That was NOT what I needed to hear. My thoughts froze, as I was walking away. I was not prepared for that answer. My teacher was being honest with me and I appreciated that. If an English teacher did not believe in dreams, who else in the school would? Suddenly, dreams seemed so far away and almost impossible to reach. I was not sure whether I should continue to believe in them anymore. People around me might laugh at me and my dreams. They might think that I must be out of my mind. I decided to put my dreams on pause and focus on my school work. After all, it would be more realistic to do well at school, so I could go to college and get a decent job in the future. Life went back to "normal". Every now and then, I looked at my dream list and the pictures that I collected. "They look so good", I sighed.

How time flies. It had been 2 years since I got the answer from my English teacher. I went to college and lived in a dorm at school. It was a tall 11 story building. In my dorm, I had 11 roommates. We all shared one room which had 6 bunk beds and 12 desks. Each of us had very limited space in the dorm, but we had a good time together.

One night, a girl next door ran into our dorm and said: "There will be a meteor shower tonight. I heard that it is the biggest one in history. Come to the top floor. Do not miss it!"

Meteor shower? Who did not like that? Let's go! I ran to the top floor and saw a lot of girls up there waiting excitedly for the meteor shower. The excitement was contagious. I got excited too.

There was an old saying that if you made a wish in front of a shooting star, then your wish would become true. This meteor shower was my opportunity, big time! Here was my plan. As soon as the meteor shower started, I would tell the shooting stars all my 7 dreams over and over again, until the shooting stars said: "Alright, fine! If you want them so badly, you can have them. Give me a break. My ears are burned out." That was my plan A, plan B, and plan C. I was determined. Fortunately, I was well prepared. Since I had been looking at my dreams for the past 2 years, I could say them backwards without a blink of an eye. I rolled up my sleeves. I was ready to "work"! There I was, waiting patiently for the meteor shower. I planned not to miss a single shooting star. Who knew how long this meteor shower would last.

Finally, there came the first shooting star. I made a wish for my first dream. Then there came another shooting star. I made a wish for my second dream. Then there came more shooting stars. I made wishes for the rest of my dreams. When I was done, the meteor shower was still on, big time. That was perfect! Let me do it all over again. It was better safe than sorry. I made a wish for my first dream, then second, then third, and all the way to the last one. Well, guess what? The meteor shower was still going strong. You know what, it did not hurt to double check. Here I came again.

It was the biggest meteor shower in history in my opinion. I had plenty of time to make wishes for each of my dreams over and over again. I did the entire process 7 times in total. That was how badly I wanted my dreams to become true.

By the time I finished, everyone else had gone. I was the last one there looking at the sky. Then there came the biggest shooting star I had ever seen. It was about 50 times bigger than a regular shooting star. It was glowing red and gold light. The scene was astonishing. I saw it in person. I made my last wish. I wished all my dreams would come true! I knew they would. I was glad that I had chosen to stay. It was too bad that everyone else went to bed and missed the grand finale.

"When you are willing to do whatever it takes,
you will become unstoppable"
- Dr. Aziz Gazipura

And you will be on fire day and night!

What Is in it for you:

Have you ever heard of The Boiling Frog Theory (Quinn, 1996)? If you have, that is awesome. In case you have not, here is what it is about. "The boiling frog is a fable describing a frog being slowly boiled alive. The premise is that if a frog is put suddenly into boiling water, it will jump out, but if the frog is put in tepid water which is then brought to a boil slowly, it will not perceive the danger and will be cooked to death (Boiling frog, 2018)."

Similarly, if your life is too comfortable right now, your urge to pursue your dreams is far less than those who struggle day in and day out for a living. It is those people who live at the bottom are more willing to do whatever it takes to make their lives better, and to achieve the lifestyle they desire. The pain of not having the lifestyle that they want has exceeded the pain to make it happen.

> "Discipline is just choosing between what you
> want now and what you want most."
> - *Anonymous*

How badly do you want what you desire? Are you willing to spend less time on TV, video games, parties, or shopping in order to make up the time necessary for working on your dreams? Are you willing to get up at 5 a.m., 4 a.m. or 3 a.m. every day to exercise and work on your dreams? Are you willing to quit smoking, alcohol, drug, or junk food so you can take charge and improve your health? Are you willing to start reading self-development books, accept where you are today, and take the responsibility to take yourself where you want to go? Are you willing to do whatever it takes?

> "*Most people get ahead during the time that others waste* (Zuck, 2009). "
> - *Henry Ford*

SABRINA Y.C. HE

"The future depends on what we do in the present."
- Mahatma Ghandi

If your answer is "YES" to all the above, then you have come to the right place. In section 2 of this book, I reveal my secret recipe of Self-Discipline. It tells how I consistently get up at 3:00 a.m. in the morning to exercise and work on my dreams every day. You do not have to get up as early as I do. As long as you are willing to take control of how you spend your time and put in the efforts to take the first baby step, my secret recipe and 6 secrets will work for you. My step-by-step guide is super easy to follow. Give it a try!

"In life, we all suffer one of two things:
The pain of discipline or the pain of regret (Rohn, Being Successful Is a Personal Choice, 2018). *"*
- Jim Rohn

3
AN UNFORGETTABLE NIGHT

"Many talented people haven't fulfilled their dreams because they over thought it, or they were too cautious and were unwilling to make the leap of faith."
- James Cameron

It had been more than 2 years since that meteor shower. One summer night after dinner, my father asked, "You're about to graduate from college. What are you going to do after that?" I hesitated for a minute. Should I tell him about my dreams? Sooner or later, I had to tell my father my plan. Why not now?

I took a deep breath and answered softly, "After my graduation, I want to study in America and get a master's degree in business." After I said that, I held my breath waiting for his reaction. I had my fingers crossed.

He was surprised. He thought for a minute and said, "America is very far away. If you get hurt or need any help, I cannot be there for you right away, at least not easily. Have you thought about things like that?"

I thought that he had a very good point, "No, I have never thought about that." I sighed.

He continued to say, "You are my only child. Everything that belongs to me and your mother will eventually be yours. I never expect you to become a millionaire or be famous someday. I just want you to be comfortable in life and have everything that you will need. I have been working really hard all these years and was able to save up some money for you to open a small shop in the neighborhood. You can sell school supplies to kids. It is a reliable business. I am pretty sure that the rest of your life will be taken care of financially, as long as you are conservative with your spending and maintain your shop well. Now, if you spend that savings to pay for a school in America, it will be gone really fast because 7 RMBs only equals to 1 US dollar. In other words, our money shrinks 7 times in America. I might be able to cover your school tuition and living expenses for a year at most. After that, you will be fully responsible for paying for everything on your own. I'm getting old, and I'm self-employed. There is no guarantee how much I can make in the future. I'm not discouraging you to study overseas. I just want you to think it over before you make your decision. Once the money is gone, it is gone. There is no going back. Whatever decision that you're going to make, I'll support you 100%."

I sat there deep in thought. I did not know what to say. It suddenly had become a bigger decision to make because it would affect the rest of our lives. I sighed, "OK. I see what you mean. Let me think about it tonight. Thank you, Dad!"

"God never gives you a dream that matches your budget. He's not checking your bank account; He's checking your faith (Larche, 2016)."
- Jimmy Larche

I went to my room and got back to my thoughts. I was sure that it was my dream to study abroad, but everything was uncertain over there. I had never been to America before. I was not sure whether I could find a job to support myself later on. On the other hand, staying in my hometown would be a safer choice because I had known this place all my life and I had family and friends here. Also, owning a small shop would give me a comfortable life for sure, because one of my aunts had owned a shop for years and her life seemed comfortable financially. However, the problem was that there was nothing exciting about that kind of life, at least to me. I could see myself getting old and die in the shop someday. It was a very sad picture to paint. I understood that studying abroad had lots of uncertainty and who knew what would happen. It could be good and exciting. It could be really bad and full of problems. It was a hard decision to make. My head started to get cloudy. I needed a break or to sleep on it, so I went straight to bed.

The next day when I woke up, I gave it more thought. If I chose not to follow my passion and pursue my dreams, I might not be really happy for the rest of my life. I would always wonder how it would be to study abroad, and what kind of adventure I would run into. I would regret for sure on the day that I die for not going for the life that I desired when I had the chance. I told my father that it was my dream to study abroad and I would like to give it a try. My father said: "OK, if that is what you want."

*"Faith is taking the first step, even when
you don't see the whole staircase. (Mirow, 1986)"*
- Martin Luther King, Jr.& Marian Wright Edelman

After almost a year of preparation and hard work, my English had improved a lot and I was accepted by a college in the United States. I was granted a student Visa for further education in Bellevue University, Nebraska. I was super excited and bought a one-way airplane ticket from China to the U.S. We had a goodbye party with breakfast in a restaurant with all my relatives on June 2nd, 2004. I would never forget that day. It was cloudy and slightly rainy in my hometown. After saying goodbye to everyone, I boarded a bus heading to the airport in Hong Kong. I sat next to a window where I could see my father standing by the curb waving goodbye. I saw tears in his eyes for the first time in my life. He looked away trying so hard to hold the tears back. I was sure that he did not want me to see it. It was sad to say goodbye, especially when we did not know when we would meet again. It could be at least 3 years from that day on, or it could be 7 years. No one knew what the future would hold.

"Real courage is being afraid but doing it anyway (Winfrey, 2012)."
- Oprah Winfrey

What Is in It for You:

Create the life that you desire and live it with joy! I refuse to bring my dreams to the graveyard. From Ecology Global Network, the statistic shows 151,600 people die every day in the world (World Birth & Death Rates, 2011). Any day could be my turn.

> *"Go for it now. The future is promised to no one."*
> **- Wayne W. Dyer**

If we do not take actions now, when? The future is promised to no one. I do not know my lifespan; do you know yours?

What are your dreams? Are you certain about your dreams? In other words, are they so important to you that you must have them come true before you die? If you do not know what your dreams are or you are not sure about them, please use the exercise in section 3 to find out your dreams. Knowing what you desire in your head will not get you there, so please write down your answers in your journal or a notebook. Take this first step. You have got this! It is easier than you think and it is a lot of fun.

If you finished the exercise, then congratulations! You took the first step towards your dreams. I am so proud of you. Do your dreams excite you? Did you dream big? Are they so big that you do not even know how to get there? If yes, then those are good signs! That means you have used your imagination, not reality.

> *"Reality is merely an illusion, albeit a very persistent one."*
> **- Albert Einstein**

Now that you have exciting dreams to go after, what are we waiting for? Let's go get them, NOW!!!!

Wait, did I hear you say that you were not ready? What is holding you back? If you worry about the uncertainty in the future after you jump, it is OK. You are human. The feeling of fear is a part of us. We all have fears. What matters is what you are going to do about it.

"F.E.A.R. has two meanings: Forget Everything
And Run or Face Everything And Rise"
- Zig Ziglar

"Everything you want is on the other side of fear"
-Jack Canfield

I have had fears before, many times. As long as I am alive, fear will be with me. To overcome fear is to go through it.

1. Write down the worst scenario that will happen. For example, I am afraid that I will not be able to pay the rent this month.

2. Accept the worst scenario. For example, alright, it has turned out to be that I am not able to pay the rent this month. I accept it.

3. How can you best take care of the situation in that scenario? For example, OK, now that I am not able to pay the rent, I can no longer rent this apartment and I will sleep in my car. I will take showers in the gym. It is not that I am going to die. I will be OK.

4. Now you are prepared for the worst and feel much better

I learned this technique from Dale Carnegie's book "How to Stop Worrying and Start Living (Carnegie, 1984)." I got the free audio version on YouTube. I highly recommend this book. The earlier you start reading his book, the sooner your life will become better. It changed my life.

"Fear is the only thing that gets smaller as you walk towards it"
- Bill Baren

Wait, did I hear you saying you do not have time? If you spend one extra hour a day to work on your dreams, you will get there in time. If you work on your dreams a little bit every day, one day you will wake up and find your dream is coming true. Be sure to check out section 2 of this book.

Facebook: 11 Dreams Go-Getter

I will show you how you can spend at least one hour a day to work on your dreams no matter how busy you are.

> *"Never give up on a dream just because of the time it will take to accomplish it. The time will pass anyway."*
> **-Anonymous**

> *"I don't have time is the biggest lie you tell yourself* (Cardone, Grant Cardone, 2016).*"*
> **-Grant Cardone**

Since the future is promised to no one, if you find you are going to die in a couple of years, how will you live differently? What difference do you want to make for society before you die? Who do you want to love more or spend more time with? What is on your bucket list?

Go get your dreams now for there is no tomorrow. Take your leap of faith and jump!

> *"It's OKAY to be scared. Being scared means you're about to do something really, really brave* (Hale, 2013).*"*
> *- Mandy Hale*

4
A CANDY SHOP IN WONDERLAND

*"Twenty years from now you will be more disappointed by
the things you didn't do than by the ones you did do.
So, throw off the bowlines. Sail away from the safe
harbor. Catch the trade winds in your sails.
Explore. Dream. Discover."*
(Brown, 1990)
- Sarah Frances Brown

After saying goodbye, I boarded the airplane to America. My adventure officially began. It was my very first time to ride an airplane. The international airplane was gigantic. It was so huge that I doubted whether it could fly. Inside the plane, I was surrounded by people of different colors, different cultures, and different languages. This was exciting. In my whole life, I was used to submerging in the ocean of Chinese.

On the airplane, I was well fed by the beautiful airline attendants almost all-day long. Fresh apples, orange juice, milk, snacks and entrees. I was pretty sure that I had gained 5 pounds by the time the plane landed in the United States. I received warm socks, pillows, and a blanket. It was so cozy. I lived like a queen during those 16-hour flight. It was an amazing experience, and I would love to do it again!

"The biggest adventure you can take is to live the life of your dreams (What Oprah Knows for Sure About Life's Biggest Adventure, 2002). *"*
- *Oprah Winfrey*

The school assigned a student to pick me up at the airport. He took me to my dorm at Bellevue University and showed me how everything worked. I learned how to turn on the shower, adjust the room temperature and how to use the oven and stovetop. I was most excited about the oven. I had never seen one or used one before. Who would have ever thought that I could make my own cake?! Life was unbelievably good. Having my own bathtub in a dorm totally blew my mind. I thought I was in a 5-star hotel. Look, I was used to sharing a small dorm with eleven other girls in college back in China. All I had to shower with were 2 big buckets of water. Kids born in America are so lucky.

I had many exciting adventures in college. I still remember my first Class. I was the first one to arrive in the classroom, and I had a hard time believing that it was really happening. In the past four years, I thought of my dreams often. At this moment, I was physically sitting in an MBA class in America like I always dreamed of. I was emotional and proud. I admired the entire room and tried to take it all in. What a special moment in my life! The class went well. I just could not get the jokes that everyone else was laughing about. "What is so funny? I don't get it! Well, first day at school. Welcome to America!" I thought to myself.

I would never forget the first phone call that I received. One day, a girl next door passed me her phone saying that someone wanted to talk to me. For me? Back then, my English was not that great, so I got very nervous when I picked up the phone. My heartbeat was so loud that I could not hear what the person was talking about. I said "pardon" at least 3 times and still could not understand a word. It was bad, and I was very embarrassed. I had a feeling that the caller was about to kill me if I asked her to tell me one more time.

The first time I explored the grocery store in America, I was amazed by the amount of canned foods on the shelves. I had never seen so many canned foods in my life. They took up the entire aisle. A lot of them looked delicious in the pictures. I wondered how they would taste. Since they were inexpensive, I picked out about thirty different canned foods to try. I was excited about my new discovery. I could not wait to check out, so I headed straight to the cashier. While I was heading out to the parking lot with the shopping cart, I realized that I would not have a ride home. I just remembered that I actually walked to the store from home alone. I guessed I would just carry the bags and walk home then. It would not be that bad, right? I found out in a hard way. I underestimated how heavy thirty cans of food could be. They were so heavy that I had to take breaks every 10 feet. It was going to be a very l..o...n..g way home. Those canned foods had better taste really good, or I would be so mad!

The first year in America, I had countless adventures. I was like a kid in a candy shop or like Alice in Wonderland. It was exciting. I was so glad that I chose to follow my dream.

What Is in It for You:

I wonder what kind of adventure you will encounter after you go for your dreams.

"It is never too late in life to have a genuine adventure."
- Robert Kurson

"Don't die without embracing the daring adventure your life was meant to be (Pavlina, 2008).*"*
- Steve Pavlina

Adventures can bring you a unique feeling of joy. It is hard to describe. You will feel it when you experience it.

5
SELF-MADE "JACKPOT"

In China, when my parents were young, they only had a few years of school education available to them. My father did not get to learn how to write, but he learned from the street and he made a good living since his 40s. My mother often told me stories about how she struggled to survive without food when she was young. My parents and I were not born rich. The picture was clear. To achieve my dreams, I had to figure things out and make my own luck.

In America, I was very grateful to my dear parents who covered my first year's tuition and living expenses. No matter how exciting the journey had been, at the back of my head, I knew that I had to look for a job and start as soon as possible. I was mentally prepared to take on any hard labor jobs available. I was willing to wash dishes in a restaurant or mop the floor if I had to.

I found a waitress job in a Chinese restaurant near my school. It was close enough for me to walk to work every day. The restaurant owner was very kind to his employees. He offered free lunch and dinner at his restaurant after work shifts. Because of that, I was able to save money from food expense and save time from cooking on my own. I spent most of my time either at work or at school. I had no time to party or the luxury to travel.

In general, tips in a Chinese restaurant are decent. Because the price of plates were inexpensive, 10-15% for tips was low. I usually made $25 for a lunch shift, and $40 for a dinner shift in a good night. I saved up every single dollar bill that I made. It usually took me 3 months to save up $3000. At the end of the third month, I handed in all my savings to the school for tuition, and then I started to save my first dollar again. Sometimes it was more challenging to be disciplined, especially when friends invited me to travel with them during holidays and summer breaks, or when they suggested trying a new restaurant in town. Oh, believe me, I wanted to go with them, but I chose not to do so. I said "NO" to those invitations, and eventually, no one invited me anymore. It was sad, but I needed to stick with my plan.

> "When you're feeling tired, dare to keep going.
> When times are tough, dare to be tougher.
> When the day has ended, dare to feel as you've done your best.
> Dare to be the best you can – At all times, dare to be (Maraboli, 2009)!"
> - *Steve Maraboli*

I worked in the restaurant for 2 years until I graduated with an MBA degree in 2006. During that 2 years, I managed to pay for all my tuition, rent and other necessary expenses. It was never easy to watch other international students go traveling and try out newly discovered restaurants. To my peers, my lifestyle was boring and plain. To me, it was worth it. I was proud of my academic and financial achievements: no student loan!

Back in China, I enjoyed watching good movies from Hollywood. One day, I stumbled into a romantic movie called "Top Gun." The main character Maverick was very charming in his pilot jumpsuit. The palm tree in the sunset by the beach was absolutely beautiful. I thought to myself that someday I wanted to marry someone like Maverick, the smart, charming and brave pilot in a jumpsuit. Guess what, I did! A few months after I started working in that Chinese Restaurant, I realized that there was an Airforce base nearby. The first time I met my future husband, he was in his pilot jumpsuit. He was so charming that I thought he was the prince from England. We had an awesome story to tell on the day we met. We fell in love and got married 2 years later.

While I studied Biology in China, my professor taught me about DNA and family disease history. He said that generally speaking, in a healthy couple, if the husband was from a region that was very far away from the region where the wife was from, then their DNA's were usually very different from each other and the chance that they had the same defect on their DNA's were low. When this couple had a child together, the child usually would have less defects and more advantages in health and other prospects. I took his theory to the extreme. If I had a baby with someone from the other side of the world, then it would be a super baby. I wanted one! In 2012, God granted my wish and gave me a super baby that I always wanted. He is beautifully mixed and is super smart. He tries to outsmart me by giving me hard times every now and then.

"All our dreams can come true if we have the courage to pursue them
(Williams, 2004)."
- Walt Disney

What Is in It for You:

When you have the courage to ask for what you really want in life, you can make it happen if you move consistently in that direction. You will get there someday. If your thoughts and actions are not aligning with that direction, then they will only be wishes.

"For every disciplined effort, there are multiple rewards
(Rohn, The Key to Getting All You Want? Discipline, 2017)."
- Jim Rohn

At this moment, in what area of your life are not happy with? Is it your health, bad habits, wasting time, not being on time, etc.? Whatever is in your way, you are capable of changing it. Taking action itself is not hard. It is simply a motion. The hard part is to get out of overthinking and start doing.

6
NO, THANK YOU!!!

> *"Time is more valuable than money. You can get more money,*
> *but you cannot get more time* (Rohn, Jim Rohn, 2013).*"*
> **- Jim Rohn**

I felt like time went by faster when I had a newborn to take care of. In the blink of an eye, 2 years had passed by since our son was born. I became a stay-at-home mom. It was a 24/7 job, on call with no vacation time or sick leave. In general, stay-at-home moms are underappreciated for their unseen hard work at home.

> *"The bad news is time flies. The good news is you're the pilot."*
> **- Michael Altshuler**

No matter how busy I was, I did not forget about my dreams. That is why listing your dreams in your journal and reviewed them often were very important. My next dream was to start my own business. Every day, when our little one was napping in the afternoon for 2 hours, I used the time to read business books. To ensure that I did not waste a single minute for learning during that precious 2 hours, I started to read as soon as our little one fell asleep in his cosy crib. Also, to ensure that no interruption would ruin the only 2 hours that I had to study, I turned off my phone and hung a sign by the doorbell. I made the sign myself. It politely said "Sh....No soliciting, please! The baby is sleeping". My underline was if you rang the doorbell, I would kill you! During the 2 hours, I learned businesses about how to get myself started. I looked at business entities, taxes and deductions, sales and marketing, real estate investment, etc. When my husband came home for dinner, I was very excited to share what I had learned that day. Each day, the more I learned, the more excited I got. I could not wait to get my business going someday. I did that for one and a half years. Around Christmas time in 2014, my husband graduated from college and got an engineering job with an awesome title "Scientist Level 1". He was full of hope and ambition to a greater future in his career. We bought a beautiful house and settled down. We were hoping that with his good salary, we could finally go travel in Europe.

After working there for 6 months, he started to see the truth. Being an engineer there was not as cool as he thought it would be. The job was not about innovation. It was not about becoming a scientist. It was all about following the government compliance to order parts for the testing which was run in the exact same way as it had been for the past 30 years and no suggestions were welcome. He also realized that most engineers there were waiting for their retirement someday. Their ambitions were dead years ago. That was NOT the kind of life we wanted. We refused to end that way. No, thank you!!! My husband decided to quit his job soon and move out of that area. I was ready for a change as well. After heavy taxes and expensive health insurance premiums, we only had $300 left each month, even though we did not have any student loans, credit cards or auto loan payments. If we wanted to have the lifestyle that we always desired, working as an engineer was not going to make it happen. We had to start our own business.

"Your time is limited, so don't waste it living someone else's life. Don't be trapped by dogma - which is living with the results of other people's thinking. Don't let the noise of others' opinions drown out your own inner voice, and most important, have the courage to follow your heart and intuition (Jobs, 2005)."
- Steve Jobs

SABRINA Y.C. HE

Summer 2015, we brainstormed with what kind of business we could have. We started with the question of what was important to our family if we had a business. We both agreed that we wanted to spend more time together as a small family. We wanted to travel to places together as much as we could. We wanted to spend more time with our son and teach him as much as we could. We wanted to have fun and enjoy life together. Based on those values, we thought that a touring business would be a great fit. My husband could be the driver and the main tour guide. I would be the assistance and take care of our son.

What Is in It for You:

Here are a few simple questions for you. Please do not overthink and just answer what comes to your mind immediately. There are no right or wrong answers.

1. When was the last time you pursued your dream?
2. What got in the way between now and then?
3. Are you settling down for less than what you want in life?
4. Is your dream still alive in your heart?
5. How badly do you still want to make it happen?
6. If your dream will become true in 2-3 years from now, are you willing to take the first step today?
7. If you do not start working towards your dream today, and you continue with your current lifestyle, daily activities, or habits, what will your future look like in 2-3 years from now?
8. If money is not a problem, how do you want to live your life?
9. If you have all the money and time in the world, how would you like to contribute to society or humanity? What difference would you like to make during your lifetime?
10. If you delay your action today and you die 3 years later due to illness or accident, what would you wish you would have done when you looked down at your coffin from heaven?

7
WENT ALL OUT FOR A WIN

The next step was to pick a great place to start our touring business. In our opinion, touring businesses in places like California, New York, Boston were saturated, and the competitors were many. It had to be a great place to raise our son, a place we would love, have a lot to offer to tourists and have great potential for future touring business. After doing some research and due diligence, we chose Denver, Colorado. To move there, we needed to sell our beautiful house. It was hard because it was our first house and we loved that place. My kitchen was gorgeous and just the way I wanted it. If we could move the house with us, we would.

A few weeks later, we sold our black hybrid vehicle for $8,000 cash. We planned to live on this cash in Colorado after my husband quit his job.

> *"Only those who risk going too far can possibly find out how far they can go (Eliot, 1931)."*
> *- T.S Eliot*

The Rocky Mountains in Colorado receive a lot of snow in the winters. We needed a special vehicle that was strong enough to climb snowy mountain roads and was big enough to carry 10 tourists with big windows to enjoy the scenic views. After some study and research, we learned that a Mercedes Sprinter with a four-wheel-drive function would be a great choice. At that time, a four-wheel-drive Sprinter was hot on the market.

Most of them were presold in the dealership, and the waiting list was long. We kept looking for one and also looked for alternatives. One day, we stumbled onto a dealership website in Massachusetts. It had a customized, brand new four-wheel-drive sprinter for sale. It had been returned by the buyer to the dealership, and it had been on the market for only a few hours. We called the dealer right away and put a down payment to hold the vehicle for us. We drove 2 days in my silver Toyota from Tennessee to Massachusetts to look at the Sprinter. The Sprinter was perfect, and we needed it to start our touring business. The dealer requested $12,000 for down payment, and we did not have that kind of cash in hand. It looked like our best option at that time was to trade in my beloved silver Toyota for the Sprinter as a down payment. I was really sad about that. The Toyota was only a couple of years old. It was a present from my father to me and I loved everything about it inside and out. To trade it in for only $12,000 was a big loss. I spent the night in the hotel to think about it. As much as I did not want to lose my Toyota, I had no other options at that time but to trade it in as a down payment. The next day, it was rainy outside. It perfectly matched how I felt inside. I could not hide the tears in my eyes. I was sad. I asked the dealer for a moment with my vehicle alone. As I was sitting inside for the last time, I sighed "I love you, my silver Toyota, I am going to miss you. Someday soon, when my business becomes successful, no matter where you will be, I will find you. I will search all over the United States and buy you back, and I am so sorry to leave you here with the dealer. I hope your new owner will take good care of you until we meet again. I love you. Goodbye." Reluctantly, I left my Toyota at the dealer and drove the Sprinter back to Tennessee.

Because we did not plan to buy a house in Colorado anytime soon, we gave away most of our furniture and gardening tools. We stuffed the rest of the furniture in a small moving pod, and packed everything necessary in the Sprinter. At around 8 p.m. in the evening, we started our drive to Denver, Colorado and left everything behind. To save money on the trip, we slept in our vehicle in the rest areas at night. Even though it was sad to leave my beloved Toyota and house behind, we felt alive for the first time for a very long time. We were finally free. We were free to decide how we wanted to spend every minute of our lives. My husband could finally spend more time with our son. We were brave and bold to take the leap of faith. Our son was a lucky kid. He got to witness and experience this journey with us. He got to spend a lot of time with his parents. The future seemed optimistic to all of us. We were so excited to get the business going. We looked forward to taking our tourists traveling and experiencing Colorado. It would be fun. We would create new memories and we would have great stories to tell.

We drove 3 days. When we finally arrived in Denver, Colorado, we stopped by a gas station to fill up diesel fuel and have a lunch. While eating our peanut butter and jelly sandwiches inside the Sprinter, we could see a beautiful and gigantic snow mountain in the distance through the big windows. What a special picnic! We felt free and fortunate. I wondered, at this exact moment, how many people felt stuck in life working at jobs that they did not like and dreaming of vacations with their love ones someday? Just a few days ago, we were in that kind of life and it was unsatisfying. I was glad and proud that we followed our hearts, took a leap of faith and went a different route from the so-called "normal" life.

"Whenever you find yourself on the side of the majority,
it is time to reform (or pause and reflect) (Twain, 1904). *"*
- Mark Twain

"Do not go where the path may lead, go instead where
there is no path and leave a trail (Strode, 1903). *"*
- Muriel Strode

It was winter when we arrived and thanks to the high-quality sleeping bags, we survived many snow storms in the Sprinter. The wind was howling outside the window, and we could see snow dumping from the sky. The roads were closed, but we stayed warm and cosy throughout the nights. The next morning after snowstorms, it was the best time to play in the snow. Our son was three and a half years old, and he had so much fun.

We lived in the Sprinter for 41 days. Every morning, we prepared parfait for breakfast in the Sprinter. After breakfast, we headed to a gym to exercise and shower. After that, we explored the city and planned where to take our tourists for a visit. We visited the capital building. We attended an Avalanche hockey game for the first time. We attended an NBA game and enjoyed the dance performance from the cheerleaders. For lunch, we made PB&J sandwiches in the Sprinter. For dinner, we usually went to Whole Food and bought a rotisserie chicken and baby carrots for less than $10. It was healthy, delicious and inexpensive. Life was really good. We were in heaven. Every day I did not have to cook or do any dishes. We hung out as a family all the time. We did fun stuff together. We worked together towards our goal for the business. It was the best time in our lives.

We had our challenges to face, but it was worth it. After a day of fun, we drove back to the parking lot of our rental storage unit. We used the public bathroom in the building to brush our teeth before bed. The code to enter the building deactivated every night at 10 p.m. That meant we had to finish brushing our teeth by then. If we needed to use the bathroom in the middle of the night, then we had to hold it till 6:00 a.m. the next morning. Brushing teeth in the public bathroom for a 3-year-old was interesting. Just like most moms, I did my best to keep our son from touching the dirty toilet or playing in the sink and then put his fingers in his mouth. Thank God that he was a great boy and listened really well.

One night, our little boy's belly did not feel well and he had an "accident" in his sleeping bag while asleep. It was mid night. We hurried up and drove to a nearby gas station to take care of the whole mess. Luckily, the employee on duty was like an angel. She understood the situation and was very kind to us.

Since we only had $8,000 in cash, we knew that we had to do something before our cash ran out. My husband came up with a plan. To supplement the income from our touring business, he planned to use the Sprinter as a limousine vehicle to make some quick cash. At night, he plugged in his laptop outside of the storage unit building to build his new business website and designed his new logo for the limousine business. Working under the street light by the sidewalk, he finished his work in a week. The website and logo turned out beautifully. From that day on, he would be in charge of building our limousine business and I would be in charge of building our touring business.

We lived in the Sprinter for 1 month and 10 days. By the end of it, we were so sick and tired of eating rotisserie chickens. We were ready to enjoy homemade meals again.

*"The path from dreams to success does exist. May you have the
vision to find it, the courage to get on to it, and the
perseverance to follow it."*
- Kalpana Chawla

What Is in It for You:

Here is a fun exercise for your imagination. We are going to time travel
into your future. Do not overthink. Just imagine and have fun. Enjoy the
process and have a great time!

1. If you take the leap of faith, what will you encounter in your adventure?
2. List all the joys you will get to experience.
3. Imagine that you are at your ideal destination doing what you love.
    What does that feel like? What are around you?
4. What are the main challenges that you will face?
5. Which challenge makes you worry the most?
6. What are you going to do to face each of your foreseen challenges?
7. After writing down your solutions, was the worst challenge as bad as
    you thought?
8. Now that you know how to face your worst challenge, let's relax and
    enjoy the moment. You are back to your ideal destination doing what
    you love. Imagine as much detail as you can. Feel it all and let it melt
    into you.

8
ELEPHANT ON A TIGHTROPE

*"The ground beneath you is shifting, and either you get sucked in
by holding on to old ways, or you take a giant step forward
by taking some risks and seeing what happens."*
- Bonnie Hammer

Since our house in Tennessee was still on the market, the mortgage payment ate up our cash really fast. It became urgent to find a job right away. After a few weeks of interviews, I got an offer to work as a linguistic software tester in an IT company. Because of this job, we were able to rent a one-bedroom apartment. To save money, we closed the storage unit and moved all our stuff into this tiny apartment. Our stuff took up the entire bedroom, so all of us slept on the living room floor for the next 6 months.

*"There are risks and costs to action. But they are far less
than the long-range risks of comfortable inaction."*
- John F. Kennedy

The company was very far away from our apartment. It took 4 hours to commute by public transportation while I worked 6-8 hours a day. To ensure that I still got to exercise and grow my business, here was how I managed to do them both as busy as I was. Every day, I got up at 4:00 a.m. to get ready for work. I put on my clothes for exercise and running shoes. In my backpack, I packed clothes to change, work shoes, breakfast and lunch. I first took the light rail train, and then transferred to a bus. I worked on our touring business on public transportation. The whole way, I wrote down business ideas, solutions and articles for our touring website, etc. It was about 1 mile from the bus station to the company. After I got off the bus, I would find a nice and safe spot to stretch and get ready for the run. The company was located on top of a hill. It was about 45 degrees uphill the whole way. Running uphill with my heavy backpack on was a very good cardio exercise for me. By the time I got to the office building, I was soaking wet, huffing and puffing. I cleaned up and got changed in the bathroom, then I was ready to work while I ate my breakfast. Some mornings, I did not feel like running, but I did it anyway, because if I did not run, I would be late for work, and that was a good problem to have. By the time I got off work, my outfit for exercise had become dry again. I got changed and ran downhill all the way to the bus station to catch the bus. Mountain weather was not predictable. It rained in the afternoon sometimes. I ran in the rain to catch my bus so I could be on time to pick up our son before the daycare closed. If I could choose, I preferred to run on a sunny day. After the first bus, I transferred to a light rail train, then took another bus and got off at a YMCA. I had 40 minutes left to exercise in the gym before I had to pick up our son from the YMCA daycare. After an intense exercise in the gym, I pick up our son and we took a bus to go home. As soon as we got home, I would cook dinner and get ready for bed as fast as I could. It was a very busy lifestyle, and I was proud that I managed to exercise and build our touring business every day. I lived like that for almost 3 months. I was in great shape.

"If you take no risks, you will suffer no defeats.
But if you take no risks, you win no victories (LEONARD, 1987).*"*
- Richard M. Nixon

Because my work in the IT company was temporary, my husband picked up a job 2 weeks after I started mine. It was a very low paying job working at the front desk for a big hotel. In case either of our touring or limousine business picked up soon, the hotel could easily hire someone new to replace him, but he would not feel too bad to leave. Due to our jobs, our son had to go to a daycare for the first time in his life. He did not like it at all, and he lost a lot of weight. His round full cheeks were gone, and he started to have a few minor health-related issues. I knew for sure that I was the one to provide the best care to our son. As a mom, it was really hard to see that our child was not happy every day. He wanted to hang out with his parents and do fun stuff together just like before. I felt bad that I could not offer him what he needed in his heart and to grow. I could hardly wait for the businesses to pick up so we could spend more time together again.

"He who is not courageous enough to take
risks will accomplish nothing in life. (Lincicome, 1977)"
- Muhammad Ali

9
WE DID NOT SIGN UP FOR THIS

As I was hoping that our business would pick up soon and I could rescue our son from the daycare, we ran into financial trouble instead. The big project from the IT company lasted for less than 3 months. The company also decided to outsource projects to Thailand. My income dropped from $4,000 a month to a few hundred. Our combined income was not enough to cover our business expenses. Our savings account was getting lower by the month. It was like déjà vu; I had to find a job quick, again. I was willing to take any job to help pay the business expenses. We needed to keep both businesses going. A few weeks later, I got a waitress job in a fancy seafood restaurant. The money was good, but my back started to hurt by carrying gigantic and heavy food trays in the restaurant. Occasionally, the IT company would pass me a few small projects to work on. On some days, I worked in the company during the day and then rushed to work in the restaurant in the evenings. I would do whatever it took to keep our businesses alive. Our businesses were our hopes.

"When defeat comes, accept it as a signal that
your plans are not sound, rebuild those plans, and
set sail once more toward your coveted goal (Hill, 1937).*"*
- Napoleon Hill

Even though we were broke, we still found ways to enjoy a day together as a family. We both worked a lot, but we had Mondays off together. We made road trips to visit different destinations near Denver, Colorado. To save money, we always packed our sandwiches in a cooler and brought lots of snacks with us. We visited Estes Park, Breckenridge, Vail and Winter Park for sightseeing. We had fun as a family even though we could not afford to spend any money in the restaurants or buy any souvenirs in the shops. Money was tight, but we had hope. We knew our businesses would take off someday soon. All we needed was to do our best and to hang in there for another year or more.

"Hope is being able to see that there is light despite all of the darkness (Solomon, 2010)."
- Desmond Tutu

The hotel took advantage of my husband's hard work and kindness. Sometimes, it scheduled him to work 10 to 12 hours a day with minimum break, food or water. When he got off work, he was always exhausted. He had lost a lot of weight since he got hired. I was very concerned about his health. I suggested he to quit his job, but he refused. He wanted to show his appreciation for the hotel management giving him a job when he needed it so badly. I saw his point, but I disagreed. I was really concerned. A couple of months had passed. One day we were on our way to visit a young couple by ridding a light rail train. On the light rail station, while we were waiting for our next connecting train, my husband got a panic attack for the very first time in his life. His head was spinning. He had a strong urge to throw up. He was shaking and could not move. He thought that he was about to die. While waiting for the ambulance, he said to me and our son: "If I cannot make it, I love you both very much." A few minutes later, the ambulance took him to a hospital. There was not enough room in the ambulance for me and our son to ride along; we were left alone on the street with a gust of cold wind. It was winter in Colorado. I did not know how to get to the hospital from where I was, so I asked people around for bus routes. A very kind lady offered us a ride to the hospital. Her name was Megan Borash, and she was an angel. By the time I found my husband in the hospital, he was hooked up with all kinds of devices. We spent hours in the hospital that evening. He finally agreed to quit his job.

Twitter: 11 Dreams Go-Getter

"The greatest test of courage on earth is to
bear defeat without losing heart (Ingersoll, 1876). *"*
- Robert Green Ingersoll

After that day, he had panic attacks more and more often. It got to the point that he could not leave the apartment. Some mornings, he could not even get up from the bed. It was the darkest time in our lives. No matter what was going to come, I needed to stay strong and keep going. I did not mind to take care of our son all by myself. I did not mind to do all the housework and cooking all by myself. The hard part was to watch him suffer in bed, and I could not do anything to help him feel better. When I worked at night in the restaurant, I had to let our son watch TV for hours until I got off work. Our poor little boy had no one to play with or talk to. His dad was lying next to him and could not move. After a few more ER visits, we received a bill from the hospital in the amount of $11,000.

My stress level was to the roof due to the financial stress, my husband's illness, the guilt of not being able to play with our son, the worries of not making enough tips at work, and did not have time to exercise for a while. One night at work, my heart started to feel bad when I lifted a heavy food tray. It was anxiety that I felt in my heart. I tried to stay strong and push through the night until I got off work, because I needed to make money to buy food. The more I resisted, the worse my heart felt. I had to stop working that night and went home to rest. I went jogging the next day to strengthen my heart and lower my stress level. Jogging helped a lot, so I did it every day until my heart felt better.

"There was never a night or a problem
that could defeat sunrise or hope."
- Bernard Williams

Due to financial stress, my immune system had become weak since I started to work in the restaurant. I got sick once a month and it happened 6 months in a row. I typically had a combination of a fever, a cold and a cough. At that time, I could not figure out why I got sick so easily and so often. Now that I look back, I understand that stress can weaken our immune system. It is important to learn how to deal with stress. Daily practice of gratitude meditation first thing in the morning will definitely help. Also, prayers and having faith will help too. Learn how to pass your burden to God and believe that when things do not go your way, you will still be OK.

"When God pushes you to the edge, trust him fully, because only two things can happen; either he will catch you when you fall, or he will teach you how to fly (I AM CHRISTIAN, 2015). *"*
-Anonymous

June 2017, we could no longer cover the expenses for both the touring and limousine businesses. We decided to close them both. We sold our Sprinter, and we lost a lot of investment on that vehicle. We had 5 credit cards to pay.

We were very sad to close our businesses. We built them from scratch. We put a lot of heart, soul and energy to grow them. They were like our babies. It was like watching our babies die. That was how sad we were.

"Winning is great, sure, but if you are really going to do something in life, the secret is learning how to lose. Nobody goes undefeated all the time. If you can pick up after a crushing defeat, and go on to win again, you are going to be a champion someday."
- Wilma Rudolph

Key Takeaways for You:

1. No matter how much you cannot stand your job, do not quit your regular job before your business makes good profits.

2. Start your business low-key. Do not invest too much money into building the business at the very beginning. Add more to your business as your profit starts to come in.

3. Do not borrow money to start a business. Be creative. There are many ways to make seed money.

4. Be prepared to fail if it is your first business. It is normal and it is a learning process. That is why it is a good idea not to put too much money into your first business. Start small.

5. Be patient. It takes time for a new business to pick up. It can take 2-3 years before making significant profits. Hang on to your regular job while working on your business. Your efforts and hard work will pay off.

6. Do not get your family involved, not even a single dollar from them. If the business fails, at least it will not affect your family member financially. Learn from my mistake.

7. Learning how to build a new business can be frustrating and stressful. Remember to enjoy the process. It is your adventure and have fun.

8. When you run into a problem, LAUGH even it is not funny. It is all about your attitude towards life. After the laugh, say this to yourself: "Every problem is an opportunity in disguise. What is my opportunity?"

9. Failure is gold. If your first business fails, never take your failure personally. Learn your lessons, forgive yourself and start a new business again.

10. "The only true failure is stop trying" --- Madame Leota (Minkoff, 2003). I wrote this down and put it in front of my bathroom mirror to remind myself every day.

10
A GOLDEN OPPORTUNITY

"Impossible is not a fact. It is an opinion
(Muhammad Ali: In His Own Words, 2016). *"*
- Muhammad Ali

After we closed our businesses, I continued working in the restaurant until we could figure out what to do next. The heavy food trays in a busy restaurant had been killing my back. Every morning I woke up with a back pain. I prayed to God for a miracle. I asked him for help to get us out of this situation, because I did not know how much longer I could hang in there.

One night, there was a birthday celebration and I was the waitress for that party. One of the guests in the party was curious about me. She said that I reminded her of her daughter. She asked me where I was from and why I was working in the restaurant. It got everyone else's attention and they started to listen. I gave them a brief introduction of myself, and they became very interested in me. A man in the party told me that he had a connection with some business owners who own more than 50 different types of businesses, and he would like to connect me with those business owners so that I could get a better job. He asked me for my phone number. I hesitated. At that moment, their food was ready to serve, so I got busy serving. While they were enjoying their dinner, I wrote down my number and kept it in my pocket. I was not sure whether that man was serious or was just being nice. When the party was over, the man came up to me and said: "Don't worry. Everyone here at the party is a doctor. We are a family. We own lots of businesses in town. With your language skill and background, we could use your help with our family businesses. This is my oldest brother." Pointing at the man right next to him, he continued to say, "He can definitely use some help with a few of his businesses." His oldest brother said: "I will call you tomorrow morning to discuss more details." He was sincere, so I took out my number and gave it to him. When I got home that night, I told my husband what had happened. He thought that it was too good to be true.

The next morning around 10:00 a.m., my phone rang. It was the phone call that I was waiting for. For identity protection, let's call the oldest brother Richard. Richard invited me to meet him in his restaurant. He would like to show me how I could fit into his businesses. We met, and I learned that Richard was a millionaire. The family I served last night had multi-million dollars in town. They owned more than 50 different businesses including restaurants, rental properties, stock investments, parking lots, vacation resorts, retail stores and on and on. I was blown away. I had never met anybody so wealthy in my entire life. I only read about them in books, like the family of Rockefeller.

Richard did not have any kids of his own. He adopted a little girl when she was a baby. She was very talented in arts but was not interested in business. He needed someone to take care of all his businesses for his wife and daughter after he passed away.

I could not believe my eyes and ears. How many people in their lifetime would run into an opportunity like this? I wanted that job very badly. I told Richard that I would love to help him with his businesses, but he was very cautious about who he could trust, so he requested to meet my husband and son. The next day, our entire family dressed up and had a family interview with Richard in his office building. Richard was very impressed with my husband who was a very handsome young man with an engineering degree and had been a sniper in the Army. Richard liked our son who was very quiet and patient during our interview. He believed that our kid's good behavior was a result of good parenting and family education. The interview went well. I was officially hired. Our family was hired. Our lives were about to be very different.

After visiting Richard's beautiful mansion, meeting everyone in his private company, and getting my own office, I officially became the CFO and senior project manager of his company. He planned to mentor me about his businesses so that I could be ready to take over someday. I was very grateful for him. He saved my back from working in the restaurant. I was grateful that I would be able to provide my family with a very comfortable life. I was grateful that I had the opportunity to learn about different kinds of businesses from him. I felt like he adopted me into his family. I planned to be loyal to his family and help his businesses to thrive. I planned to be there for them for at least 10 to 20 years.

A week later, Richard took our family to visit his private ranch house. He owned the entire canyon in that area. We lived and ate like kings there. Every day was a new adventure for our family. It was so wild that it took us a month to calm down and accept what life had brought us. We only shared our story with families and close friends. They could not believe what had happened to us. Some of them called it a fairy tale of Cinderella in real life. We were so blessed.

"My mission in life is not merely to survive, but to thrive; and to do so with some passion, some compassion, some humor, and some style (Angelou, 2011)."
- Maya Angelou

11
HAPPILY EVER AFTER?

A few weeks after I got hired, Richard offered a job opportunity to my husband. It was a temporary project, but if he could pull it off, he would have an opportunity for a permanent position down the road. My husband accepted the challenge. He worked day and night for that project and was able to pull it off just in time, and Richard was very impressed with the result.

Meanwhile, in order to support my husband for his project, I took care of our son, took over all the cleanings and cooking, and worked very hard at my new job. During the final stage of his project, the lease of our apartment was up. My husband insisted on moving to a bigger apartment while I thought it would be better to wait until the project was over. He had a strong will, and I had a soft heart. We moved. While he was busy with the project, I ended up busy with unpacking, looking for a good school for our son and learning new things at work. It was quite a lot of new things to figure out all at once and all on my own. Because I worked too hard both at home and work since I got hired, I caught bronchitis and coughed like crazy. The week that I got sick, Richard was out of town. I went to work in the office as usual, but one lady in charge requested I go home until I got better. At that time, I was also in charge of marketing for Richard's restaurant. Due to my cough, I could not go to the restaurant to work neither. Usually, coughing took weeks to heal. Without the internet in the new apartment, I could not work at home neither. I was in a very tough spot.

"Life has many ways of testing a person's will,
either by having nothing happen at all or by having
everything happen all at once (Coelho, 2008).*"*
- Paulo Coelho

A week later, Richard returned from his trip. He was not happy about the complaints against me in the emails that he received. He told me that some people in the office and restaurant believed that I was not a good fit for the company. He planned to give my job to my husband so that I could stay home to heal my cough and take care of our son. I was shocked by his decision, because I did not see this coming. I worked hard, and I planned to be there for his family for a very long time. What did I do wrong? I went home and told my husband that I lost my job. He was not surprised. Richard talked to him a few days ago and asked him to consider taking over my position. I was almost the last one to find out. My head was spinning. My world was spinning.

I was so sad that I lost my job. After crying for a few days, I started to comfort myself and look on the bright side of the situation. It was not the end of the world. I just need to figure out what I did wrong and how I could do better next time. Maybe this was a good opportunity to focus on taking care of our son and catching up with some house work. Maybe it was a good opportunity to write my book. Our family income would drop slightly, but we would still be comfortable because Richard agreed to pay my husband with the same salary as I earned before. I was mentally ready to become a stay-at-home mom again. I was confident that I would thrive no matter what I do.

Life is a box of chocolate; you will never know what you are going to get. A week after I lost my job, my husband asked for a divorce before he went to work. I was shocked. I could not believe my eyes and ears. My world turned upside down. Could someone please explain to me what was going on? I could handle losing a job. I could always find a new one. But I could not handle losing my marriage. It could not be casually replaced. What about the tough times and good times that we went through together in the past 12 years? What problems did I have that I could not possibly fix? What happened to the promise that we would be buried together when we died in our old age?

My heart was bleeding. I cried for 3 weeks. I was willing to change and do whatever it took to save our marriage, but he believed that our marriage was hopeless and he refused to stay in it any longer. My last hope was crushed. I fell in the United States, and I fell hard.

"Nobody deserves your tears, but whoever
deserves them will not make you cry."
- Gabriel Garcia Marquez

Key Takeaways:

1. Having a job is equally as risky as having your own business. You can lose either of them, but in business you have more control.
2. You can choose to be loyal to your job, but your job may not return the favor.
3. Happily ever after does not exist in real-life marriage.
4. A healthy marriage takes lots of maintenance and learning.

If you like this book so far, or if you learn ONE thing that is new, please leave me a review. If you leave me a 5-star review, please share this book with anyone you think would benefit from it. Thank you for your help to spread my mission!

12
RETURNED TO
THE SAFE HARBOR

"Life takes you to unexpected places.
Love brings you home (McClone, 2013). *"*
- Melissa McClone

With a broken heart, I flew back to my hometown in China with our son, little Benjamin. It had been 7 years since I visited China. I had my wedding reception last time I visited. Ironically, this time I visited due to the divorce. It was so nice to see my parents, my family and my friends again. It was a sensation of warmth and welcoming. I was surrounded by love which I needed desperately.

I did not tell many people about the divorce. I did not want to talk about it at all. It was too hard for me to mention it without crying. Maybe in a few years down the road, I would be able to announce the divorce after my heart healed. This time I only told my parents and a few others. I requested them to keep it a secret for now.

I planned to change for the better and learn from my past. I started to read books again. While I was puzzled as to why I lost my job and my marriage, I searched and searched until I found a book that pointed out my issues that I needed to work on. It was called "Not Nice" written by Dr.

Aziz Gazipura. I learned a lot about myself from his book (Gazipura, 2017). I wished that I had learned about the pattern of how I think 20 years sooner. Every day, I read books to sharpen my mind and worked out to strengthen my body. Also, the love from my family helped me to heal. I thought to myself: "Someday I will fight back. I refuse to be defeated forever."

My parents' door was always open for me to come home. They had been waiting for 14 years since the day I headed for America to pursue my dreams. This time, my parents did not want me to go back to America because I no longer had a home to go back to. They believed that I would be better off in China to start a new life. They were right about that. If I stayed in China, life would be very good and comfortable for me. Everything was in my favor. I could easily make plenty of money and get to travel anywhere I wanted to go. I would have families and friends around all the time. I would have great food to eat anywhere I went. Benjamin would be very popular in school for sure because he was handsome and he could speak English like a native speaker.

A month went by fast; it was time to pick a direction. Should I stay in China or go back to America? What would you pick if you were me? To most people, it was obvious that I should stay in China. It was a no-brainer decision to make. In America, life would be hard to start all over again as a single mom. I did not have any immediate family support around me. I did not have cousins or close friends nearby. I had to look for a job to pay rent; I did not have any savings in the bank. I had lots of debts to pay off, and half of the time I had a young child to take care as a single mother. All the odds were against me if I chose to go back to America. The picture would not be pretty. Challenges would be awaiting me there.

It was a big decision to make. I slept on it every night. At the end, I decided to go back to America. I fell hard there, and that would be exactly where I would get up again. I refused to flee out of America because I was defeated. I went there to fulfill my dreams, and that would be how it would end! I was ready to go against all odds. A warrior would not be defeated forever; there would be a day that she would return to fight for victories. Sorry, my dear parents. I had to go back to America to finish what I started. I would make you proud. I would make myself proud. I would be back!

Website: 11DreamsGoGetter.com

"Chase your dreams but always know the road
that'll lead you home again (McGraw & Douglas., 2006). "
- Tim McGraw

Key Takeaways:

1. Our broken hearts can be healed, but it takes time, family love[2], physical exercise, gaining new knowledge, and efforts.
2. We are actually stronger than we think.
3. When we decide to take FULL responsibility for whatever has happened to us in the past, we learn and grow dramatically.
4. Self-pity will keep us in the past. Get rid of it as fast as you can.
5. We are not stuck. We always have a choice in our attitude and direction.

---

[2] "family love" is not always biological. Not everyone has a family that they can count on, but your family can be people who you choose, who have energy that gives you energy and can fill you up with the love and support you need to regain your strength.

Twitter: 11 Dreams Go-Getter

13
THE HUMAN SPIRIT IS HARD TO KILL

"Tough times never last, but tough people do (Schuller, 1984).*"*
- Robert H. Schuller

May 6th 2018, I landed in Denver International Airport with little Benjamin. We were back in America. By that time, my ex-husband had already moved out to a new place. My old apartment would never feel the same again. Meanwhile, our joint bank account had a $0 balance. My dear parents gave me $2000 to help me get back on my feet. I truly owed them everything.

"Well, any good comeback needs some true believers (Boehner, 2012).*"*
- John Boehner

My ex-husband already paid rent for our old apartment for that month and left me all the furniture. Every little bit helped. The $2000 from my parents would not last for long in Denver, Colorado. My rent alone was almost $1500 a month. That meant I had 25 days to get back on my feet. I had to find a job, quick. Whenever Benjamin was at school or with his dad,

I would be busy working on my resume and cover letter. The question was what kind of job should I apply for?

A long time ago, I learned somewhere from a book that if I want to be successful, I need to start from sales. Sales skills are essential for any success. I came back to America to be successful. That was my goal, and I would do whatever it took, even sales! Also, a sales job would provide a platform for me to approach and practice talking to strangers every day until I could overcome my discomfort of making conversations. No matter how much I did not feel like approaching strangers, I had to do it to earn any income. For these 2 reasons, I was certain that a sales job was what I needed to achieve success and overcome my social anxiety.

Immediately, I started to apply for sales and marketing companies. Much to my surprise, it was really easy to get in because most people hated sales jobs. Within 2 weeks, I got 3 interviews and 3 offers. That moment felt good.

"I have always said that everyone is in sales. Maybe you don't hold the title of a salesperson, but if the business you are in requires you to deal with people, you, my friend, are in sales (Admin, 2009)."
- Zig Ziglar

What Is in It for You:

People love to watch comeback movies. Why cannot we live in our own comeback movies? This is my comeback movie, and I am the director, producer and main character.

Sales jobs may repel you, and I totally understand. It is a tough job, and especially, no one likes to take more rejections after tons of rejections. As a matter of fact, even if you do not hold the title of a salesperson, every one of us is a salesperson in life. For example, parents sell their ideas to their kids the way they want their kids to behave. We sell ourselves in a job interview to get the job that we want. We sell our spouses on the ideas of eating out tonight or going to the movie theatre. Whether we are aware of it or not, we are all salespersons. People are selling everywhere and all the time. A sales job will officially teach you sales skills, persuasion skills, communication skills, listening skills, and how to build self-confidence. To succeed, start with a job in sales because the skills that you will gain from it will set a solid foundation for your future success.

14
THE COMEBACK POWER

Part 1: Learning New Skills

Within 3 weeks after I returned to America, I started the sales job. The job was 100% Commission, and I was very scared. Doubts started to creep in. What if I could not make enough to buy food and pay my bills? The financial stress and worries about the future gave me anxiety. On the other hand, I was afraid to approach strangers because I believed that nobody liked to be approached by salespeople. Guess what? I used to run away from salesmen in the mall! No matter how much sales repel others, sales was a great way to find out what I needed to work on and improve. Issues like anxiety, worries, fear of rejection, self-doubt surfaced every day at work. It was very challenging, but I needed it, and it was good for my growth.

"Be willing to be uncomfortable. Be comfortable being uncomfortable.
It may be tough, but it is a small price to pay for living a dream
(McWilliams, 1994). *"*
- Peter McWilliams

To overcome my social anxiety faster, I needed to take massive action which was to approach strangers over and over again at work. Typically, I approached 120 strangers, and got 115 rejections on a daily basis. I worked 5 days a week. If you do the math, I approached 2760 strangers and got 2645 rejections in just one month. After working for 3 months, I approached 8280 strangers and got 7935 rejections. Now I could call it Massive Action.

"Rejection is more valuable than inaction.
All that I have learned until now has been because of rejections.
Inaction didn't teach me a thing (Agnihotri, 2019)."
- Neeraj Agnihotri

When I just started my sales job, I had a hard time to start working right away, because I really did not want to get all the rejections awaiting me ahead. Honestly, who in the world would like to get his or her feelings hurt? It took a big person to take rejections in a professional manner and not personally. There were days that I sat in my car in the parking lot at work for at least an hour or two to gather courage and overcome anxiety before work. Occasionally, people gave me dirty looks or yelled at me to go away. That hurt the most! "Be nice!!! I had feelings, too!" I thought to myself. Sometimes I had zero sales at the end of the day which meant that I did not make a penny for the entire day. I thought about quitting so many times, but I did not quit. I chose to stay because I wanted to be successful, and the nature of this job was like a cold turkey stuffed with tough love. It was good for me. It was never easy to start with, but the more I practiced and the more I learned, the more sales that I made. After taking massive actions at work for less than 3 months, I was transformed into a brand-new person. I became a better, stronger, bolder version of me with tons of confidence. I no longer took rejections personally. I started to enjoy talking to strangers and making them laugh. Who could resist a wonderful human being like me?

"Destruction comes before creation; we must say
goodbye to the old to welcome the new."
- Anonymous

Part 2: The 3 S's to Achieve My Dreams

My 3 S's were Self-Investment, Self-Discipline and Self-Love.

SABRINA Y.C. HE

Self-Investment:

"The most important investment you can make is in yourself."
- Warren Buffett

When I first started my sales job, I did not know much about sales skills and I earned very little. To make ends meet, I started to learn subjects related to sales skills as many as I could. There was no free time to waste. I was constantly learning. I listened to audio books when I was driving or doing dishes. My first paycheck was only $380. It started to increase as I learned more. One month later, my sales performance was in first place among all our companies in the country. Learning became fun. I looked for more books to read. I became obsessed with self-development. Life was exciting.

To learn more, I attended seminars and events. Soon I realized that some free seminars were set up to sell me expensive classes. They did not care much about my growth and education. They cared more about my money. I could learn just as much from reading a book for less than $20. There are many good books to read and learn. When you choose a book to read, especially a self-help book, make sure that the author really exists, in other words, they are not written by ghost writers. Also, make sure that the author has done what he or she is teaching in the book. If you do not want to buy books, there are free resources to learn as well, like going to your local library, online videos or articles, etc.

"The more I learn, the more I realize how much I don't know."
- Albert Einstein

Self-Discipline:

I learned that most successful people get up early in the morning to meditate, exercise and learn. A good morning routine sets the tone for the rest of the day. I needed to test something out and build my own morning routine. I started with getting up at 5:00 a.m., and it was not enough time to finish all the steps of my morning routine. I changed it to 4:00 a.m. and learned that I could finish my morning routine, but I was always half an hour late for work. I then changed it to 3:30 a.m. It was better, but I could not finish a full physical exercise. I finally changed it to 3:00 a.m., and it worked like a charm. I was almost guaranteed to have enough time to meditate, exercise, and learn before Benjamin woke up for school. However, when he got sick and woke up at 3:30 a.m. in the morning, I did not get to do my morning routine at all. That was a part of being a single mother. Otherwise, no excuses were acceptable.

"I don't have time is the biggest lie you tell yourself (Cardone, Grant Cardone, 2016)."*
- Grant Cardone

To ensure that I got up at 3:00 a.m. consistently, I requested an accountability buddy to hold me accountable. Here is how I did it. I sent a text message to my accountability buddy at 3:00 a.m. when I got up. Because a smart phone showed the time when my text message was received, the information on the phone would prove that I got up on time even the phone was on silence. Also, to ensure that I would not go back to sleep after I sent the text message, I texted my buddy again at 4:00 a.m. when it was time for me to read a book. Then to ensure that I would not fall asleep while reading, I texted my buddy again at 5:00 a.m. when it was time to do physical exercise. I did all that for 30 days straight and then I continued for another 30 days. Sometime during the second 30 days, my new schedule had become my new habit. I no longer had to text my buddy 3 times in the morning. I only sent one text message to my buddy at 3:00 a.m. because I knew for sure that I would read and exercise for sure after I got up. By the end of my second 30 days, I no longer had to text my buddy at 3:00 a.m. any more. I only sent one text message to my buddy sometime during the day, just to let my buddy know that I got up on time and finished my morning routine that day. Right now, getting up at 3:00 a.m. is my solid habit and a part of me. I just do it day after day. I no longer need to text my buddy any more.

I continue to improve my mooring routine. For updates, please email me at 11DREAMSBOOK@GMAIL.COM. Maybe you can join me online

Website: 11DreamsGoGetter.com

to exercise together. Honestly, what is the chance that you know someone in your life to work out with, who gets up as early as I do and exercise every day? Come join me! I will send you the link to join me if you email me.

Please check out section 2 in this book. I reveal all my secrets to build a long lasting and consistent self-discipline habit.

"Work hard at your job, and you can make a living. Work hard on yourself, and you can make a fortune (Rohn, Jim Rohn, 2017).*"*
- Jim Rohn

Self-Love:

"Sometimes we are so generous with our love, so willing to give it all away, we leave nothing behind for ourselves (Faudet, 2017).*"*
- Michael Faudet

I had learned self-love the hard way. When I was married, I sacrificed all my energy, efforts, time, money, love and almost everything for my husband and my son. I put their needs before my needs. I called it love. Well, the problem was that I had a hard time being happy because my own needs were not met. When I was not happy, it affected the quality of my marriage. As a result, a divorce was the end.

"Never make someone a priority when all you are to them is an option (Maya Angelou: In her own words, 2014).*"*
- Maya Angelou

"I've really come to realize you have to love yourself before you can expect someone else to (JOHNSON, 2014).*"*
- Leah Remini

Divorce did not seem like a fair outcome for all that I had sacrificed, but it set me free. It taught me an important life lesson of self-love. Only when I learned how to love myself, care for my own needs, and pursue my dreams, could I better love someone else. When my needs were met, I could be happier. When I became happier, I could become more attractive, and people would want to be with me more.

"It takes a deep and abiding love for yourself to have the patience to wait for the companion who is mentally healthy enough to see the beauty in your heart. No filters required (Autherine, 2018).*"*
- J. Autherine

Key takeaways:

1. If you want to change your job but do not want to go back to college, then take a sales job for a change. The new skills you will learn from sales jobs will open so many doors for you.
2. *"Insanity is doing the same thing over and over again and expecting different results* (Pickle, 1981).*" – **Anonymous***
3. If you feel stuck in life, then it is time to expand your ability by learning new things, reading books and developing new skills.
4. College graduation is not the end of learning. It is the beginning of self-learning. The good news is that you do not have any homework or exams to worry about. You can pick any subject to learn at any time. It is exciting and fun.
5. I know you have work and family to care for. Do not forget to take care of your own needs first. When you pursue your dreams and fulfil your needs, you become happier. That would expand your capacity to love others around you.

Instagram: 11 Dreams Go-Getter

6. When you give yourself permission to take care of your own needs first, you are actually giving other people permission to take care of their own needs first in their personal lives. Life will be easier for everybody and everyone will be happier.

BONUS

If you have a broken heart from your previous relationship, there are a few YouTube videos that I highly recommend watching. They will help your heart to heal and move on with greater ease. You will have less hard time to be alone at this particular stage of life. Hope you find them very helpful as well.

1. If You Love People More – Watch This, by Jay Shetty
2. If You've Been Hurt – Watch This, by Jay Shetty
3. If They Left You – Watch This, by Jay Shetty
4. Be Someone Who Makes You Happy, XoXo, by Jay Shetty

Here is a meditation that I used before bed to help me to move on. I was fully present during this meditation and I let all my feelings out. I cried a lot during the meditation and I felt wonderful the next morning. I only needed to use it once. It helped me to move on. With all my heart, I wish you all the best!

- Breaking Up – Healing & Closure from a Broken Relationship Spoken Meditation, by Jason Stephenson

15
THE LONE WOLF

"It is better to walk alone in the right direction than to follow the herd going in the wrong direction."
- Anonymous

The day that I decided to come back to America, I knew that I would face loneliness a lot and I would have to deal with all the problems by myself. When things did not go my way, I felt lonely and helpless the most. "Why did I choose to come back?" I sighed. One night, I got off work late. I was driving on a highway alone. It was late and quiet. I wondered if I died unexpectedly at this moment, how long would it take for someone to notice? How long would it take for someone to notify my parents in China? Was it really worth it for me to stay in Denver and fight alone? The apartment was dark and quiet when I got home. I craved for a hug, a kiss or comfort. I was attacked by loneliness too many times. It was very tempting to be in a new relationship during hard times.

"The time you feel lonely is the time you most need to be by yourself (Coupland, 1993).*"*
- Douglas Coupland

To deal with loneliness, some people choose to get into a new relationship not long after they broke up or divorced. It is called a rebound relationship and it rarely lasts. A few people choose to work on themselves so they can learn from the previous relationship and grow to better themselves. If we do not change ourselves, we will attract the same type of lovers and get the same results like before. I chose to reflect, to learn and to grow. At this particular stage of life, I needed to learn how to be happy when I was alone. This was a new lesson that life was trying to teach me. I made myself a commitment that I would not date anyone for 2 years since the day my ex-husband asked for a divorce which was on March 7th, 2018. I needed to focus on learning, growing and pursuing my dreams. Since I made this commitment, there have been some cute guys that have shown up in my life and asked me for dates. Temptation worked really hard against my plan. It is hard to stay focused and I prayed for strength. I put this commitment in my book so all my readers could hold me accountable. I wanted to and needed to stay focused. It is good for me.

"When you choose to take the road less travelled, it can sometimes be a bumpy ride along the way, but if you're doing it for the right reasons, then the reward is so great (Bleiler, 2010). *"*
- Gretchen Bleiler

Everybody has dreams, but 99% of them are not willing to do whatever it takes to make their dreams happen. As you progress in learning and working towards your dreams, you will notice more people around you are willing to settle down with what is easier to get. You will notice more people like to follow others like sheep in the herd and they like to complain. They could be your loved ones or friends. As you grow, the gap between you and them will get bigger. It is going to be hard for you to leave them behind. Please do not blame yourself and accept the fact that everyone is on his or her own journey. Everyone has his or her own timing. Some will start to learn and grow later in their lives. Some will never learn or grow until they die. It is OK for you to move on. You have dreams to achieve. You have a difference to make. You are in the 1%, and you are the one and only one to make your dreams happen.

"A lot of people like to complain, but they don't want to do anything about their situation. It's necessary to get the losers out of your life if you want to live your dream. It is necessary to know that everybody won't see it., that everybody won't join you, that everybody won't have the vision. It is necessary to know that you are UNCOMMON breed. It is necessary that you align yourself with people and attract people into your business who are hungry, people that are unstoppable and unreasonable, People who are refusing to live life just as it is, and who want more. That people who are living their dreams know that if it is going to happen, it is up to them."

- Les Brown

What Is in It for You:

Please let me introduce a very good friend of mine: Femi Olasupo. She has victories facing loneliness. She plays this game at a whole other level. I invited her to share her insights and methods, so we can help someone who feels lonely and is having a hard time being happy on his/her own. In order to achieve a solid and wonderful relationship down the road, we believe that before you look for a new relationship, it is better to wait until you have your life figured out, know what you really want in life, and are able to bring out the best in yourself. Meanwhile, we hope that your future partner will be doing the same, learning, and growing on his/her own. When you both are better equipped, you both will be able to give to each other, help make big dreams come true and take life to a higher lever together.

I appreciate her valuable inputs. Please check out her secrets in section 3 of this book: How to face loneliness and feel truly happy on your own, written by Femi Olasupo.

16
A BURDEN OR A GIFT

*"I believe that whatever comes at a particular
time is a blessing from God."*
- A. R. Rahman

7 years ago, it was the week of Christmas in 2011. I prayed and asked God to give me a healthy, happy, handsome and sweet boy. September 2012, I received exactly what I asked for. Baby Benjamin was born. He was perfect and exactly what I wanted. I was very grateful for this precious gift from God.

I became a stay-at-home mom and spent a lot of quality time with little Benjamin. He had been very sweet until he started kindergarten. With other kids' influence at school, he brought home some naughty behaviors. He was slowly but surely turning into a rotten egg and I could hear my grey hair growing.

Along with the divorce and the struggles to make a living, these problems were magnified. I was lonely and felt helpless. Benjamin was ungrateful for things that I did for him, and he gave me hard times often. There were nights that I cried in my bed. I was depressed and frustrated.

"Life is 10% what happens to you and 90% how you react to it
(Swindoll, 2006)."
*- **Charles R. Swindoll***

Some parents leave their kids to the grandparents after the divorce, because they want a fresh start. I kept Benjamin with me when it was my turn, but there were times that I regretted getting married and having a child. Because of those kinds of thoughts and attitude, our relationship got worse. He kicked my leg when I pick him up from school, and I did not like him much neither. We both were hateful and ungrateful. That lasted for months.

Finally, I was sick and tired of being frustrated and unhappy. I could not live like this for any longer. It was painful, and it was not fair to him. He did not ask to be born. I brought him into this world, and it is my responsibility to give him love and more love. I had to find a way to change the situation.

"The mind is its own place, and in itself can make
a heaven of hell, a hell of heaven (Milton, 1667)."
*- **John Milton***

To change the situation, I needed to change the way I looked at the situation. I needed to think differently. Maybe I could thrive again even I was a single mom. Maybe I could be more creative and positive to get the most out of this messy situation. I needed to believe that we could be happy again, even if it is just the two of us. I needed to believe that we still could make our lives colorful and full of sunshine, even though my ex-husband was out of the picture. I wanted to believe that we both could learn and grow together. I started to believe that I could raise him to be a great man who was happy and had big dreams. Little Benjamin needed me more than ever. We could rebuild a strong bond between us, like how we used to be. I would like to spend as much time as I could with him, to cuddle him, read him books, to play and laugh together. I would kiss his cheeks as much as I could and tell him how much I love him as often as I could. He was still my best present from God. I was very grateful to have him in my life. Love was what I needed to heal, not a new husband.

Twitter: 11 Dreams Go-Getter

After relentless efforts, our relationship got better by the day. One night before bed, he told God that I was the best present to him and he was grateful. It felt so good to hear that. Thank you, Benjamin.

Whatever comes my way, it is not a burden; it is a gift.

What Is in It for You:

If you are a single parent, I understand your daily struggles and how you feel. It is not easy. The divorce or breakup is our past; we cannot change what has already happened. However, we can change our attitude towards our situation.

"We cannot go back and start over, but we can begin now, and make a new ending. (Sherman, 1982)"
- James R. Sherman

Being a single parent is not only the end of the previous relationship, it is also the beginning of a new journey. A journey of self-growth and giving more love. When we give love, we receive love. Love and time will heal our broken hearts. The more love we give, the faster we can heal. When we master the art of how to get the most out of any situation with gratitude, we will realize that we have become a better version of ourselves. We will be stronger, healthier, smarter and happier. The hard times in the past are our blessings.

"Life doesn't happen to you, it happens for you (Carrey, 2014)."
- Jim Carrey

Instagram: 11 Dreams Go-Getter

17
SON, LET'S GROW TOGETHER

It was about time to pick up where I left off and make the rest of my dreams come true. To practice the visualization technique that I used before, I collected new pictures that looked close to my dreams, and displayed them in front of my bathroom mirror because the more I got to see the pictures, the better.

Little Benjamin saw the pictures for the first time when he walked in. He was surprised and asked: "Mom, what are those?" pointing at the pictures in front of my mirror.

Me: "Those are pictures of my dreams and things that I want to do."

Benjamin pointed to one of the pictures and asked: "Uoo...what's this?"

Me: "This is Disney world. I want to take you there for fun someday."

Benjamin: "Disney world? It looks fun there. I'm so excited!"

Me: "Me, too, buddy. I cannot wait."

After that night, he always came up with new questions to ask me whenever he saw my pictures. They were the cutest questions ever and I enjoyed them.

One night, he asked: "Mom, do you know what my dream is?"

Me: "What is your dream, buddy?"

Benjamin: "I want to play basketball someday."

Me: "Oh, is that what you want to do? You know what, buddy?"

Benjamin: "What?"

Me: "Maybe we can find a picture of a basketball player dunking the ball in the net, and put it in front of your bathroom mirror. What do you think?"

"Yeah!!!" He shouted with excitement

Me: "What else do you dream about doing?"

Benjamin: "Uhmm...I don't know yet."

Me: "I see! If you think of anything that you really would love to do, just let me know. We will find the pictures together and put them in front of YOUR mirror. Does that sound good? "

Benjamin: "OK, mom. I cannot wait."

I never thought that my dream pictures in front of my mirror would have such a great impact on little Benjamin. I never expected much from him when he grew up. I just wanted him to be happy, healthy and to pursue his big dreams.

The more I learned, the more I could share with little Benjamin. There were many life lessons that I wished I learned about them when I was younger. At least now I could teach them to Benjamin when he was only 6-year-old. What a great start!

18
MORE TO COME

By now, you probably are eager to find out what my dreams are. Here is a peek to my dream list:

- ✓ 1st Dream: To live abroad and experience a different culture
- ✓ 2nd Dream: To get an MBA degree in America
- ✓ 3rd Dream: To marry a charming prince of my life
- ✓ 4th Dream: To have a beautifully mixed super child
- ✓ 5th Dream: To start my own business
- ✓ 6th Dream: To write & publish my book

I started to write this book in 2013. I wrote a few chapters and then I stopped writing for years. Why? Because I had self-doubt. I worried that people would laugh at my life stories and tell me that my stories were meaningless. I planned to wait till my 60s or 70s to write, then I certainly would have better stories to tell and more value to offer to the readers.

Now that I look back, I am very grateful for the hard times that I had earlier this year. It was emotionally painful. It was dark and hopeless. I was frustrated and lonely. Yet, from the struggles, I have stretched and grown a lot since. By learning new things, reading books, taking massive actions, being disciplined, and facing my fears, I have become a brand-new person. I am stronger and better. Now, I am aiming to achieve my next dream.

My 7th Dream: To achieve financial freedom

I hope my story has inspired you to pursue your dreams, most importantly to take actions, massive actions. Reading my book is just the beginning. You have to do your part. I cannot do it for you. Remember that time will pass by no matter if you take actions or not, so do not waste your life. Tomorrow is not guaranteed, thus now is the time to go for your dreams. Do not bring them into your graveyard like the majority! Today, take your first step which is to simply follow my step-by-step guide and do it every day. That is all I ask. It is just that simple and easy. Do it for 30 days continuously and watch your transformation. You will be amazed.

May all your dreams come true!
Love

Sabrina Y.C. He
Englewood, Colorado, USA
On Christmas Day
December 25th, 2018

The following was added for you on Sunday, June 7th, 2020.

My original plan was to make my 7th dream come true which was to achieve my financial freedom first, and THEN to write a book to reveal how I did it. The book would be a guidance for you to achieve your financial freedom which would set you free from working a 9:00 – 5:00 job and living paycheck to paycheck. In other words, you could finally devote your energy, time, heart and soul to your dreams, so that your heart will be filled with fulfillment and joy, and you can make a difference to society.

A successful entrepreneur and author, Gary Vaynerchuk, mentioned in his book "Crushing It" that the journey of achieving success could provide more value for people than the result of the achievements. He wished that he had recorded his entire journey as he was working towards his success so that other people could get the most out of his success story. His words made me rethink my original plan.

Because it usually takes 3 -10 years to achieve financial freedom—and I would love to provide valuable contents for you sooner—I have decided to replace my plan and reveal my progress LIVE on social medias. You can find me by searching "11 Dreams Go-getter, Sabrina" to instantly find out the new actions that I have taken, the new rejections that I have just faced, the new mistakes that I have made, the new lessons that I have learned, and the small victories that I have tasted. I believe that my journey will help a lot of ordinary people like me, who were not born with silver spoons in their mouths, who are struggling to make ends meet, feel exhausted from running endless daily errands and still want to make their dreams come true eventually.

If you follow my journey, you will get to experience my ups and downs, and you may be so inspired by my actions that you decide to take actions as well. Wouldn't it be wonderful if you have made your dream become a reality by the time that I have made my 7th dream come true?

Come follow me! (Please search for "11 Dreams Go-getter, Sabrina")

Great job! You just have finished section 1 of this book. Before we move on, I have a favor to ask.

If you like this book so far, or if you learn ONE thing that is new, please leave me a review. If you leave me a 5-star review, please share this book with anyone you think would benefit from it. Thank you for your support to spread my mission!

SECTION 2

MY SECRET RECIPE TO SELF-DISCIPLINE

1
THE 3 A.M. LION

Lions wake up early to go hunting for their food. They attack the day early because they are hungry. How hungry are you for your dreams?

My favorite question to answer is when people ask me what time I get up in the morning. I am glad that they ask. I like to answer casually, "3 o'clock", pretending that it is no big deal. It is fun to get to watch people's facial reactions. Their shocking reactions are the best compliments to me.

"Not everyone will understand your journey. That's fine.
It's not their journey to make sense of. It's yours
(Dean, Not everyone will understand your journey, 2013)."
-Zero Dean

What drives me to get up so early? That is a very good question. To accomplish my dreams is my drive. A couple of my dreams are missions to accomplish. These missions are bigger than myself. I want to touch millions of people's lives, to inspire them to follow their hearts, and to pursue their dreams. The world needs more people "alive". I want to show them the way by doing it myself first. I walked the walk, and then I will talk the walk. It is quite opposite from "talk the talk and walk the walk." It is worth it for me to be very disciplined because I have souls to save. They are waiting for me to show them the light in the darkness and to light up the world soon. Like Grant Cardone says: "We are in a hurry to serve (Cardone, Be Obsessed or Be Average, 2016)!"

Facebook: 11 Dreams Go-Getter

If one day I die unexpectedly, I will absolutely be kicking myself if I did not try to make my dreams come true while I still had the chance. I will regret that I did not look my best, that I did not free my soul to pursue what I love, and that I did not experience all the wonderful things that the world offers. When I still had the chance, I could have laughed more, loved more and experienced more.

If one day your life suddenly ends without any warning, what will you be kicking yourself for not doing when you still had the chance?

"Why live an ordinary life when you can live an extraordinary one."
-Tony Robbins

2
THE FORGOTTEN PRINCIPLES

There are things that we know are good for us but we choose not to do them in our daily lives. Every day is made of little choices. Some people continuously make poor choices. Guess what, little poor choices add up fast. We are the one to blame for the situations we are in today whether it is in finance, relationship, or health. It is time for us to stop blaming our circumstances and to take full responsibilities for our lives, so we can take ourselves to where we want to go.

Some good knowledge or principles have been around for thousands of years. We know them all along but we choose to ignore them because we know them by our hearts. We just do not apply them! If you desire to take your life to a new level, the bad news is that you may want to seriously consider applying the principles. The good news is that they are easy to follow. We can start with using the principles as guidelines when we make little choices throughout the day. Remember, your life is formed and shaped with all little choices that you make every day. Take control of your life by taking control of little choices. Here is how I do it. Every morning, I listen to my beast-mode-on-demand playlist so that the motivational messages can become a part of me. If you do the same, you will start to notice that it gets easier to make better choices in your daily life. The playlist is in section 2, chapter 5, Magic Potion: Beast Mode on Demand. Now, let's get to the 3 basic principles.

Principle No.1:
Start the Day with A Good Morning Routine Every Day

A good morning routine sets the tone for the rest of my day. After I finish my morning routine, I feel energetic, productive, proud and unstoppable. I also gain a great sense of accomplishment because I already have finished my exercise and worked on my dreams before most people get out of their bed.

I have learned to appreciate the importance of my morning routine from days that I could not do it because little Benjamin got sick and woke up at 3:30 a.m. in the morning. As a result, I had low energy and I dragged to do anything for the rest of the day. I made poor decisions on food choices. Negative thoughts and worries crept in my mind easily. By the end of the day, I had not much accomplished, and I felt drained, like a walking dead.

That is why I strive to do my morning routine every day and keep my fingers crossed that little Benjamin or I will not get sick.

Principle No.2:
Get Enough Sleep Every Night & Take A Cat Nap During the Day

Getting enough sleep is very important. It sets a solid foundation and preparation for an effective execution of next day's morning routine. I have noticed that when I sleep for less than 7 hours, I have a hard time waking up in the morning. I feel tired and I drag myself to the gym. I end up with an unsatisfied exercise and I easily have negative thoughts throughout the day. I am less efficient, and it takes me longer to accomplish anything.

When I have 7 hours of sleep, I wake up naturally before my alarm clock goes off. I can easily get out of the bed and I am ready to conquer the earth. I feel energetic and it is easier to get into beast mode during my exercise. I work out hard, I move faster, and I feel great after my awesome exercise. For the rest of the day, I am creative and optimistic. I perform better at work. Having enough sleep makes a big difference.

The goal is to get 7 hours of sleep and to do the morning routine every day consistently. Since I get up very early, I usually take a cat nap during the day for 15-20 minutes so I can recharge my energy. The nap is short but it is powerful. It helps me to maintain high productivity for the rest of the day. In case you wonder, I do not drink any coffee or energy drink. I do not need them and I choose not to use them. A nap is all I need and it solves the root cause of tiredness.

Principle No.3
Drink Plenty of Water

1. Our brain is composed of 73% water (The Water in You: Water and the Human Body, 2019). Water helps our brain to function better, thus we can be more productive and make better choices.

2. A dehydrated body will have a more difficult time to exercise in the gym.

3. In case that you are just wondering, the answer is "No, soft drinks and coffee do not count." Drink water, plenty of good old-fashioned water!

3
THE COMPOUND POWER
OF BABY STEPS

Please understand that it is a process, BUT it does not mean that it is going to take forever. It means that it needs consistent actions in order to notice the big change. Also, it takes time for your body to adjust itself to the new schedule. For example, if you are used to getting up at 6:30 in the morning, do not try to get up at 3:00 a.m. right away in the next morning. Instead, change your schedule gradually. You can start from getting up at 6:00 a.m. every day for a week, then get up at 5:30 a.m. for the second week, get up at 5:00 a.m. for the third week, and 4:30 a.m. for the fourth week and so on, until you get used to getting up at 3:00 a.m. every day. Once you have become used to getting up at 3:00 a.m., please keep it consistent and get up at 3:00 a.m. every single day, because getting up on time one day and sleep in the next day will confuse your body and your body will feel tired easily. Keep it consistent then your body will get used to the new schedule, and you will not feel tired when you get up (Assuming that you slept for at least 7 hours the night before). Do not confuse your body by not getting up on time. Consistency is the key.

To make sure that you do not go back to bed after you turn off your alarm clock, keep your alarm in a different room next to your bedroom. That way you can still hear your alarm when it goes off, and you will make yourself get up and walk a little bit to turn off the alarm.

When it comes to forming a new schedule for your bedtime, the same idea applies. If your bedtime is 10:30 p.m., you can start from changing it to 10:00 p.m. for the first week. After that, change it to 9:30 p.m. for the second week and then change it to 9:00 p.m. for the third week and so on, until you will have 7 hours of sleep for sure before your alarm goes off the next morning. It also means that you need to learn how to say "NO" to invitations for late night parties. Your sacrifice and self-discipline will pay off when you are living your dreams in the near future while those party owls are still stuck in life. To ensure that you can go to bed on time, it is important to make plans two hours before your bedtime arrives. For example, what time do you need to start and finish dinner, what time do you need to brush your teeth, etc.

To nail down a good routine for your morning and night time, it takes trials and errors. Keep adjusting along the way until you can be in bed on time and get up on time consistently.

4
DARE TO BET

I had been wanting to finish writing my book for a long time. I reached to a point that I became sick and tired of not having my book finished. I got stuck in writing and I felt discouraged. Sometimes my self-doubt was so strong that I almost gave up finishing writing this book, but writing my book had been my dream and I was determined to make it happen.

There is a technique called "burn the bridge" or "burn the boat". By using this technique, you will put yourself in a situation which you can no longer back out easily but to move forward towards your goals. Here is how I used this technique in order to finish writing this book. It worked! One day, I was in a large gathering for an event. I announced to a big group of guests that I was going to finish writing my book within 3 months. If I failed to make it happen, I would give away $100 cash to every single guest in that group. When I made that announcement, I was near broke and I certainly did not have that kind of money to give away. The best way out was to start working on my book immediately and to have it finished by the end of the 3rd month since the event. As a matter of fact, that was how I started my 3:00 a.m. morning routine and I have been getting up at 3:00 a.m. since then. As a result of using that technique and getting up super early to write my book, I finished writing my book within a month. At that time, my book was a "vomit" version of everything in my mind. It needed a lot of editing, but at least I finished writing my book 2 months ahead of deadline.

I used the power of accountability to ensure daily execution of my plan which was to get up at 3:00 a.m. every morning, so that I would have enough time to exercise, learn and write my book before I headed out for my job. It was very helpful to have an accountability buddy when I just got started. Think about it, if no one held me accountable, I could write a rain check for myself whenever I felt lazy. Conversely, knowing that someone was expecting my report of daily execution, I took it more seriously. I did not want to disappoint my accountability buddy, and I wanted to be a good role model for my buddy as well, so I kept my words and just did it. To make it really work, I purposely picked a buddy who was on the same path to grow and who would agree to take no excuses from me.

Here is a review of how I used accountability on a daily basis. To ensure that I got up at 3:00 a.m. consistently, I sent a text message to my accountability buddy at 3:00 a.m. when I got up. Because a smart phone showed the time when my text message was received, the information on the phone would prove that I got up on time even the phone was on silence. Also, to ensure that I would not go back to sleep after I sent the text message, I texted my buddy again at 4:00 a.m. when it was time for me to read a book. Then to ensure that I would not fall asleep while reading, I texted my buddy again at 5:00 a.m. when it was time to exercise. I did all that for 30 days straight and then I continued for another 30 days. Sometime during the second 30 days, my new schedule had become my new habit. I no longer had to text my buddy 3 times in the morning. I only sent one text message to my buddy at 3:00 a.m. because I knew for sure that I would read and exercise for sure after I got up. By the end of my second 30 days, I no longer had to text my buddy at 3:00 a.m. any more. I only sent one text message to my buddy sometime during the day, just to let my buddy know that I got up on time and finished my morning routine that day. Right now, getting up at 3:00 a.m. is my solid habit and a part of me. I just do it day after day. I no longer need to text my buddy any more.

On the other hand, to make sure that I would go to bed early and have enough sleep at night, I sent a text message to my accountability buddy every night when I was 100% ready for bed. My bedtime used to be 10:30 p.m. By repeating the process of going to bed 30 minutes earlier than the week before, my new bedtime is now 8:00 p.m. I owe my buddy a big hug for helping me when I got started.

Since then, I have improved my morning routine. Because sometimes little Benjamin woke up during my physical exercise, it was challenging to finish my work out while trying to get him ready for school at the same time. Therefore, my new morning routine starts with gratitude meditation, then followed by physical exercise, and then followed by writing or learning. It has been working really well.

5
THE MAGIC POTION: BEAST MODE ON DEMAND

Many people want to exercise on a regular basis, but only a few people have actually done it. Why? Because most of the time, we do not FEEL like exercising, even though we know that it is good for us to exercise more often.

Beast mode can take over most of the lazy feeling. You will have a great exercise if you can get into a beast mode. Here is how I go from trying to wake up early in the morning into a beast mode.

1. Preparation: the night before, I get my outfit ready for next day's exercise. Note: No baggy clothes for exercise, please!!! Baggy clothes kill the mood. To help you get into beast mode faster, select outfits that make you look like an athlete, a superhero or a superheroine. Outfits make a big difference.
2. Nobody FEELS like exercising right away after waking up. Start from getting changed into your clothes for exercise and putting on your running shoes.
3. Listen to motivational videos and upbeat music while you are stretching and loosing up your stiffness in the gym.

4. Continue listening to motivational videos and upbeat music throughout your entire exercise.

I have a playlist that I listen to during my exercise every day. It is about 2 hours long and it is a mix of motivational videos and upbeat music. I have learned that if a playlist only has music, it will be hard for me to get into beast mode fast, or to get through tough sections of my exercise. If a playlist only has motivational videos, I will miss listening to music after a while and tune out from the motivational messages. My playlist has been working really well for me, especially during hard sections of my exercise.

I listen to this playlist every morning when I exercise. By listening to the same motivational videos every day, I have the messages burned into my brain. Whenever I do not feel like exercising, my brain instantly reminds me of those motivational messages word by word. Now it is hard for me not to be motivated because those motivational messages have become a part of me. This is the magic power of repetition.

In case you need recommendations, I am going to share with you a part of my playlist. If I discover a better motivational recording or song, I will update my playlist. For that reason, I invite you to follow my YouTube channel (11 Dreams Go-Getter) for my latest Beast Mode on Demand playlist.

1. Music: Stronger (What Doesn't Kill You) by Kelly Clarkson.
2. No Excuses – Best Motivational Video, posted by Ben Lionel Scott.
3. No More Excuses – Motivational Video, posted by Mulligan Brothers.
4. Music: Happy by Pharrell Williams.
5. I Will Not Stop – Powerful Workout Motivational Video, posted by Marvis M.
6. No Excuses – Best Motivational Video 2017, posted by Motiversity.
7. This Is for All of You Fighting Battles Alone (Walk Alone Speech), posted by Team Fearless.

Website: 11DreamsGoGetter.com

8. Music: Warrior (feat. Lights) by Steve James.

9. I Can, I Will, I Must – Motivational Workout Speech 2018, posted by Alex Kalts Motivation.

10. Unbroken – Motivational Video, posted by Mateusz M.

11. Dream – Motivational Video, posted by Mateusz M.

12. When You Feel Like Quitting – Remember Why You Started, Posted by Team Fearless.

13. Music: I Smile – Kirk Franklin.

14. Stay Focused – Motivational Video Compilation for Success in Life & Studying 2017, posted by Motivation2Study.

15. Music: Endless Love Music Video – Pumpin Blood (2014).

16. Lone Wolf – Motivational Video for All Those Fighting Battles Alone, posted by Team Fearless.

17. Confuse Them with Your Silence and Shock Them with Your Results, posted by Team Fearless.

18. 20 Principles You Should Live by to Get Everything You Want in Life – Master This! Posted by Team Fearless.

19. Everyone Needs to Hear This – Find Your Passion, posted by Jay Shetty.

20. 10 Keys to Success You Must Know about – Take Action Today! Posted by Team Fearless.

21. How to Deal with Loneliness - #Believe Life, posted by Evan Carmichael.

There you have it! Listen to this playlist every morning when you exercise. Do it for 30 days straight and then continue for another 30 days. You will be on fire day and night.

6
MY STEP-BY-STEP GUIDE

To ensure that I get to exercise and work on my dreams before little Benjamin wakes up, I dedicate the first few hours in the morning to myself. I use that time to focus on my health and self-development, because they are crucial to my future success. I have learned not to underestimate the compound power of daily repetition. Here is what I do every morning.

1. At 3:00 a.m., I get up and immediately put on my outfit for exercise

2. I brush my teeth while listening to Morning Gratitude Affirmations. I repeat the gratitude messages softly.

3. I switch to my playlist for exercise and start to stretch/warm up in the gym

4. I spend one and a half hours to do a full exercise which includes stretching, maintenance, strength training / cardio.

5. After my exercise, I get a glass of whole milk and take a quick shower.

6. After shower, I spend about 2 hours[3] working on my dreams. At this point, it is to write this book

7. Last, I wake up Benjamin, get him ready for school, and get myself ready for work

In case that you need recommendations for morning gratitude affirmations, here are a couple that I listen to first thing in the morning. Listening to morning gratitude affirmations or doing morning gratitude meditation is a great way to start a day. This habit will gradually improve your life for the better and you will feel happier. Here is my morning gratitude playlist on YouTube.

• Morning Gratitude Positive Affirmations, posted by Unlock Your Life
• Morning Gratitude Affirmations 1 Listen Every Day!!! Posted by Law of Attraction Coaching

Please do not check your social media on your smartphone or computer until you have finished all your morning routine. It is very crucial not to fall into the temptation of checking your text messages and social media. Your morning routine is your priority. Everything else can wait and will go nowhere. Your focus and discipline will pay off.

---

[3] 2 hours is just an example. On days that it is my turn to take care of little Benjamin, I have 1 hour and 15 minutes to work on my dreams before I wake him up for school. After I drop him off at school, I spend 2 hours and 30 minutes to work on my dreams before I go to work. On days that my son is under the care of my ex-husband, I spend 5 hours and 30 minutes to work on my dreams before I go to work. On my day off, I usually work on my dreams for 8 to 12 hours. I believe that the more time I spend to work on my dreams, the sooner they will come true.

7
THE 30 DAYS RULE

It takes 27 days to replace an old habit with a new habit, but I like to take an extra step just to be safe. I use 30 days as my guideline to form and strengthen a new habit. After the first 30 days of doing my morning routine consistently, I aimed for another 30 days. To this point, my morning routine is no longer new to me. It has become a part of me. It has become my solid habit. Consistency and repetition are keys to form a new habit in order to replace an old one.

My biggest thrill to get up at 3:00 a.m. in the morning is that I start and finish my exercise when it is still dark outside. The stars in the sky are beautiful. The breeze sings through bushes and trees. It is so quiet and peaceful. The gym in the club house has become my personal gym at these hours because the equipment is immediately available for me to use. I love everything about my morning routine! I work hard for hours when everyone is sleeping. I know for sure that I am getting ahead by the day.

8
EVERYONE HAS ISSUES

When you give yourself "reasons" why you cannot do it, you are blocking your mind to possibilities. When that happens, examine your own statement carefully. It is important to be able to tell the difference between facts and opinions, and it takes practice to build that muscle. For example, as a single parent, it is almost impossible for me to find time to work on my dreams while raising my kid because I am too busy. In this case, "I am a single parent" is a fact. "I raise my kid" is a fact. "It is almost impossible to find time" is an opinion. "I am too busy" is an opinion because no one holds me at gunpoint and forces me to spend my day in a certain way. How to spend my day is purely my choice to make.

"I am the master of my fate, I am the captain of my soul (Henley, 1888). *"*
- William Ernest Henley

Everyone is in a unique situation. Everyone has issues to deal with. What matters is that what you are going to do about it. Life does not happen to you; it happens FOR you. Your circumstance is what makes you special. It gives you unique value to offer to this world.

"Every problem is an opportunity in disguise"
- John Adams

You may think that I have become calm and cool all the time whenever a problem comes up. No, absolutely not. There are times that I struggle, times that I feel frustrated and times that I am impatient. The difference between the old me and the new me is that the new me has more self-awareness and I am able to catch my own negative reactions faster. When I feel frustrated, I ask myself this question: What is the new lesson that life is trying to teach me? When I struggle, I remind myself that every problem is an opportunity. What is my opportunity? When I worry, I remind myself that whatever comes my way, it is not a burden; it is a gift.

Everyone only has 24 hours a day, so spend your time wisely. Life is made of time. When time is gone, a portion of your life is gone. No money or gold can buy it back. Please choose to spend your precious time working on what will really improve your life in the long run. Doing dishes and folding laundry can wait. They are going nowhere. To save time, I cook one meal that can feed us for 3 days so that I do not have to cook often. I stack dishes in the sink and only do dishes when I run out of clean ones. I have a pile of clean laundry waiting for me to fold patiently. Am I lazy? Absolutely NOT! Do I lack organization skills? Certainly not. Before my divorce, I used to keep my place sparkly clean all the time. That got me nowhere. I used to cook fancy meals every night for my family and ended up doing dishes all night. Now I choose to live differently. Simple is better. I choose to spend my time wisely. Achieving my dreams will dramatically improve my life in the future, so I have decided to spend more time working on my dreams every day.

9
WHEN YOU FEEL LIKE QUITTING

This may come as a surprise, but believe me that there are times when I feel like quitting and giving up. Afterall I am human. When I get the urge to quit, I immediately stop any activities that I am doing and find a place where I can be alone. I will either sit down or lay down where I can relax comfortably. Once in my comfortable position, I close my eyes and take a deep breath. I start to focus on my feelings and try to be fully present in the moment. I ask myself a few questions. Why do I feel like quitting? Why am I overwhelmed? What is overwhelming? Does the source causing me to be overwhelmed align with my heart and passion? How would I handle the situation if I follow my heart and passion? Does my solution energize me? Life is simply too short. As human beings, we are happiest when we live according to our own unique style. Life is a journey sprinkled with what seems like never ending challenges. Even so, let's remind ourselves to have fun and learn to enjoy the journey. All our journeys are unique. We all have a lot to learn, discover and grow.

I sometimes do not look forward to doing challenging exercise in the gym because I believe it is going to be difficult. The more I believe that it is going to be difficult, the more resistance I feel. I need to immediately shift the way I think in order to finish my full exercise and feel proud of my accomplishments when I leave the gym. I say to myself, "It is a piece of cake. All I need to do is to count how many repetitions I am doing. It is easy. I have got this." With this attitude, I have often finished my full exercise with flying colors.

When I feel like quitting, I remind myself why I started in the first place. When my time has come and I am lying in my coffin reflecting on my life, I will absolutely be kicking myself if I did not try to make my dreams come true while I still had the chance. NOW is the time. THIS moment is my second chance to fight for my dreams and to make them happen.

If somehow none of the above methods work on a particular day when you feel like quitting, here is the least that you can do. It is super easy. Go on an intense walk while listening to the motivational videos that I have listed in "Beast Mode on Demand". You can have the intense walk either on a treadmill, indoor track or outside. The key is consistency. Do it every day and do not skip a single day.

10
THE NEW CHARACTER

Earl Nightingale once said: "If you spend an extra hour each day of study in your chosen field, you will be a national expert in that field in five years or less." This statement changed Jim Rohn's[4] life, and it is about to change mine. Imagine, if I spend 2 extra hours each day to work on my dreams, then I will have my dreams come true in less than 3 years. If I spend more than 2 hours each day, then my dreams will come true sooner. As early as I get up to work on my dream, I plan to give it 18 months. All of my hard work and self-discipline will pay off by either achieving my dreams or transforming into the person I want to become.

"Self-discipline is a key to many doors.
Not least of which is one that leads to a better, stronger,
and healthier version of yourself (Dean, Lessons Learned from The Path Less Traveled, 2018). *"*
- Zero Dean

---

[4] Jim Rohn was an American entrepreneur, author and motivational speaker. He was born on September 17th, 1930 in Yakima, WA. He passed away on December 5th, 2009, in Los Angeles, CA. Retrieved from https://en.wikipedia.org

11
THE 6 SECRETS

Warning: Do not attempt to skip the stories and jump right into this section. There is a reason why these 6 secrets are close to the end. Skipping sections 1 & 2 will reduce the power of these secrets. It is like making a pot of chicken soup without the chicken. If you did not skip anything, then let's reveal the secrets

- Secret #1 Be very certain about your dreams
- Secret #2 Have a mission bigger than yourself & want to make a difference
- Secret #3 Have faith, know that it is going to happen
- Secret #4 Do not take defeat personally
- Secret #5 Make time to be alone & do my morning routine everyday
- Secret #6 Dare to bet, burn your boat and bridge

These are my 6 secrets to a consistent self-discipline. I have achieved great results by applying them. After the first 30 days of doing my morning routine, I started to see changes both physically and mentally. I became healthier, happier, highly productive and more focus on achieving my dreams. I liked the new changes and I wanted to keep them up. I made it to 60 days, and then 90 days! I was obsessed with the new me. I want to be consistent with my routine for the rest of my life while continuing to improve it and make it better.

SECTION 3

TOO GOOD TO MISS

1
A PLEASANT EXERCISE: THE STEPS TO FIND YOUR DREAMS

I cannot stress enough about how important it is to find your dreams and to be certain about your dreams. When you must have your dreams come true before you die, self-discipline becomes easier. Dreams are your powers to move forward.

Here are the preparations and steps to find your dreams. Follow your heart and feel your feelings. Remember, no dream is too big. Let's get started.

1. You need some alone time. It can be a weekend by yourself ideally, or 2 hours each day if you work 3 jobs to survive.
2. Find a quiet place where you will not be interrupted by anyone for a long period of time.
3. Turn off all your devices, especially your cell phone. Put them away where you will not see them.
4. Have a journal, a pen and a bottle of water ready.
5. Find a comfortable spot to sit down where you can let your imagination go wild.

6. If knowing for sure that all your dreams will become true, how do you want to live your life?
7. Who do you want to become?
8. What are your fantasies that you desire and you are willing to trade your life for?
9. Imagine that you did not live the life that you desire and you are lying in your coffin right now. If heaven gives you a second chance to live again, how will you live differently?
10. Remember: "Life is too short to be little (Disraeli, 1844)." - **Benjamin Disraeli**
11. "If you can dream it, you can do it (Fitzgerald, 1980s)." – **Tom Fitzgerald**
12. Pick one of the following areas that you want to start with and focus on: Finance & Material Life, Spiritual health & Mind development, Physical appearance & Health, Parenting, Social Life, Career Life, Dating & Relationship, Social Contribution.
13. Finish one area at a time. Please do not jump to the next area until you answer all the following questions within the current area.
14. For your information, some questions take longer to answer because we are going to dig into our heart and soul. Sometimes it takes time to figure out what we really want in life. It is OK. The answers have been in you all along. We just need to put them in writing. It took me an entire week to finish mine, and it is worth it.
15. For each area that you pick, please answer the following questions:

   a) What do I want in this area?
   b) Why do I want them this way?
   c) What will happen if I do not achieve them?

    d) Why am I passionate about them?

    e) What pleasure will I gain in my life if I achieve them?

    f) What pain will I feel in life if I do not achieve them?

    g) How can I achieve them? (Strategies. Not detail plans)

16. When you finish one area, move on to the next area. Answer all questions from a) to g) for the new area.

17. When all the areas are finished, look for pictures resembling your vision in mind. You can find them in magazines and cut them out, or you can find them online and print them out. Try to have pictures for all areas above.

18. Display all the pictures on a clipboard or on the wall where you can see them every day. I display mine in front of my bathroom mirror. I see them every time when I use my bathroom.

19. Do all the above once a year for adjustments or changes.

I learned most of these from Tony Robbins[5]. If you need more details, you can check out his video about setting goals and then come back to finish the above exercise. Here is the name of his video on YouTube.

"Tony Robbins: How to Achieve Any Goal You Want (Tony Robbins Motivation), posted by Law of Attraction Coaching"

After you have fully completed the above exercise, I recommend you listening to a guided meditation to help you visualize your desired future. I use it every night as I fall asleep to reprogram my unconscious mind. It is called "The Power of Creative Visualization" by Lisa Nichols.

---

[5] Tony Robbins (born Anthony J. Mahavoric; February 9, 1960) is an American author, entrepreneur, philanthropist and life coach. Retrieved from https://en.wikipedia.org

2
HOW TO FACE LONELINESS & FEEL TRULY HAPPY ON YOUR OWN
WRITTEN BY FEMI OLASUPO

Introduction: Please let me introduce a very good friend of mine: Femi Olasupo. She has victories facing loneliness. She plays this game at a whole other level. I invited her to share her insights and methods, so we can help someone who feels lonely and is having a hard time being happy on his/her own. In order to achieve a solid and wonderful relationship down the road, we believe that before you look for a new relationship, it is better to wait until you have your life figured out, know what you really want in life, and are able to bring out the best in yourself on your own. Meanwhile, we hope that your future partner will be doing the same, learning, and growing on his/her own. When you both are better equipped, you both will be able to give to each other, help make big dreams come true and take life to a higher lever together. I appreciate Femi's valuable inputs. Enjoy!

We all go through stages of loneliness while we are either waiting for the love one to show up, or grieving for the love that we thought was meant to be once it leaves. However, there is a big difference between being alone and being lonely. Being alone requires inner peace and a developed sense of self-love. Feeling lonely comes from believing that you or your life is lacking in some way, and that the best way to solve it is through something external.

You may wonder how you can face loneliness while being alone. That is a very good question and I am here to help. I understand that it is not easy to get through the discomfort of loneliness, but it is possible to not feel lonely while being alone. As a matter of fact, you can even feel truly happy while being alone. I have practiced the following methods for years and they have worked like a charm. I have benefited so much from these practices that I am excited to share them with you. Let's get it started.

1. Get clear on all the qualities that you would love your potential partner to have, and then...BECOME THAT. It is not fair when you ask your partner for something that you are not willing or capable of giving. For example, if you desire someone who is kind, start being kind to others. If you desire someone who is rich, start learning how to improve your finance. If you desire someone who enjoys travelling, start travelling on your own. Do you see the pattern here? You are likely to bump into people who have the ideal traits that you are looking for, by doing the activities that they have been doing!

2. Tap into your feelings over anything else. If you close your eyes right now and imagine that you are with the love of your life. You are walking down the street, holding hands, engaging in a great conversation, and smiling at one another. How does that feel? Describe that feeling in detail. Here are a few examples. What do you smell? His cologne or her perfume. The scents of a park or the smells of a city. Describe it all. What is he/she wearing? What are you wearing? Why did either of you pick that outfit? Maybe you love seeing him wearing that shirt because you gave it to him for his birthday. Maybe you are wearing a shirt that shows your shoulders because you know how much he adores you in it. Feel all the feelings that comes along with. As you walk, how is he/she looking at you? When you are talking, what does he/she look like when listening? When he/she is talking, what does he/she look like? Tune into all the things that you love.

The important thing is to really feel it and be there! It is called visualization. The practice of visualization always helps me live in a future moment RIGHT NOW as if it is happening for real. The most awesome thing is that your brain really does not know the difference between real and unreal. Whatever you see in your mind and really focus on, your brain thinks that it is real and then sends real signals down to your body, so you are actually capable of being in the state of being in love with your significant other RIGHT NOW. This is a game changer because there is no need to wait. You can have all these delights that you want right now. The crazy thing is that the more you tune into this, the more you will attract all that you desire towards yourself.

Imagine doing this exercise before going to a social event. You have just spent 15 glorious minutes with the love of your life. Now when you walk into the event chances are your posture will be that of someone in love, you will likely be smiling ear to ear, and you will interact with people as if you are on cloud 9 because you are! Your brain cannot tell the difference, remember?

Now, let's say, you just spent all week at home alone feeling lonely and throwing yourself a pity party every night. Each night you are at home alone, watching sad movies, crying, eating Cheetos on your couch and barely moving. You committed to going to this social event, so you begrudgingly put on some clothes, not the best outfit because who cares, you are going to die alone, right? You drive to the event and walk in.

What do you think your energy is like in this scenario vs the other one? What about your posture? Are you even smiling? How will you interact with other people? From a place of joy and fullness or lack and unworthiness?

It may sound silly but energy is everything and the "film" we play over and over in our head is not just make believe, it is the blueprint for the life we are creating.

It is 100% OK to feel lonely. In fact, it is 100% OK to feel every emotion. However, you are the CEO of your own life and if you are complaining about feeling lonely and not being with someone, and you are not working on building the qualities in yourself that you hope to attract, you are not taking ownership over the energy you bring to the moment, then I have bad news for you: who you are and what you want are out of sync!

3. Get your needs met. Often, I think people are lonely not because they truly want the honor and privilege of being with someone, getting to witness the growth and becoming of another human being, or even to add value to the life of another person. Typically, people want to be in a relationship because:

   a) You think a relationship is what you are supposed to be in ("supposed to" is a very bad word by the way, right up there with "should").
   b) You caught the comparison bug, and all your friends are hooking up, in a relationship or getting married so something must be wrong with you if you are not getting married, too!
   c) You need external validation that you are worthy, and you have the misguided belief that a relationship will provide this for you.
   d) You want sex.

You will notice that there is no focus on what you can give or add to the life of another person in any of those reasons. Some might argue, no, what I really want is:

Connection, deep connection with another human being.

To that, I call BS! Because you can cultivate a deep connection with family, friends, and new people at any time. You do not need to be in a relationship with that. If you have a genuine need for a connection, there are plenty of ways to fill that need without being in a relationship. You have only convinced yourself that the only vehicle by which to receive connection is a romantic relationship. If the connection is truly what you seek, how often are you reaching out to the people already in your life with the intention to deepen that connection? How often do you initiate making time to connect with those people or even new people? I would guess you are sitting on a gold-mine of connection and you are not exploring that because you have convinced yourself that it must come from a romantic source.

Instagram: 11 Dreams Go-Getter

Get really honest with yourself and answer 2 questions:

1) What do you truly believe you want or need from a romantic relationship that you are not getting right now?
2) If nothing in your life will change in terms of finding a romantic partner, what will you do or change in order to be happy now?

For example, if you want someone to go on trips with - invite people to go on trips with you! If you have a need for physical touch, get a massage or maybe volunteer with animals.

The point is you are spending so much time and energy living a lesser life because one aspect is not the way you want it to be. You are overlooking all this power to take the reins of your life and direct it toward the feeling you ultimately want and that you previously thought could only come from a romantic relationship. What if you could be happy now? What if you could get all your needs met by taking creative and inspired action? Are you willing to at least try or do you prefer to cling to your own unhappiness? At the end of the day, the most powerful thing you can do to lift yourself up and change your life is CHOOSE. We can only control our own thoughts, choices, and actions. We cannot make people fall in love with us, but we can choose to create a life that fills us with so much excitement and joy that our happiness becomes contagious! And, you know, that is a really attractive way to live.

4. Be the Party.

When you choose to take control over only that which you truly have control, something shifts. You become the party. That means you make it your mission to fill your life only with the people and things that light you up, reflect back to you that you are good enough, and make you glad to be alive! It changes your state so that you have more moments of high energy than low energy. It is the idea that you are a living party. You are a party, and the party you are at only gets better and better the more you learn and grow. This party is AWESOME and no matter who comes and goes from the party - meaning the people you meet, friends, romantic interests, etc. - the invitation and opportunity are the same:

Hey, I am having an amazing party, and I would love to see if you are a fit for my party. Let's hang out!

They hang out and no matter what happens, if they stay a while or a long time. If they never make it to the party or if they stay with you for years and years at the party; dance and laugh through sickness and in health until the party and all its awesomeness kills you. The point is you were already having an incredible time!

Loneliness shows up because your party sucks. Loneliness shows up because you do not even want to be at your party. But guess what, you have the power to change that!

Be your own party. Get to the business of populating your life with things that make you feel like no matter what, even if I have to dance at this party alone forever; there will be a smile on my face and so much gratitude in my heart because of how much fun I am having! Be so full of life, love, and gratitude that you have no choice but to overflow with value and generosity of spirit, and anyone who even walks past your party cannot help but stop and see what it is all about.

We cannot control who comes into our lives or who chooses to leave.

Be the party so that no matter what, you know that you are enough, that you are having a great time, and that you are in good company no matter who else shows up to the party. Just in case you need ideas on how to make your party better:

- Take a trip you have always wanted to take
- Join social groups
- Take yourself out to dinner and a movie
- Call a good friend who you have not talked to in a while
- Call a friend you talked to recently
- Invite someone new to do something new
- Do something creative you enjoy but never make time to do
- Do something physical you enjoy but never make time to do
- Cook a beautiful meal or take a cooking class
- Go for a walk around your city and pretend to be a tourist
- Do a staycation in your home or at a local hotel

- Curl up with a good book and a cup of tea
- Take a bubble bath
- Clean your home and possibly redecorate
- Journal
- Put on some great music and dance as silly as you want to
- Practice doing something new with your makeup
- Take a long drive and talk to yourself and sing super loud
- Do an adult coloring book and listen to music
- Look up bloopers on YouTube to your favorite comedy show
- Watch a comedy special online or go to a live comedy show
- Go to bed early and sleep in
- Exercise
- Treat yourself to a massage
- Look up free events in your city and go to one - try striking up a conversation with someone new while you are there
- Go to a shopping mall, and people watch
- Look at the ceiling and fake laugh for 30 seconds, really do it! This is a Tony Robbins technique. See if you do not start really laughing.
- Stand in a power pose for 30 seconds - change your body, change your state
- Attend a new class somewhere nearby
- Listen to inspiring talks on YouTube
- Craft an inspiring talk and deliver it in the mirror
- Write a list of 50 compliments to yourself
- Write 3 things you are genuinely grateful for right now

When in doubt, just grab one of these and get your party started! If like attracts like, then loneliness attracts loneliness. And as logic would have it, a happy, fun, single person committed to living an abundant and full life no matter what will attract exactly that. This is your life. It will not last forever, and you deserve to be happy. Happiness is not and has never been dependent on anything outside yourself. Be the party and create your own happiness now."

3
AN INTRODUCTION TO SELF-LOVE
WRITTEN BY FEMI OLASUPO

Introduction: Self-love builds a strong foundation to your future success in any area. It is important to accept and love yourself for who you are. Self-criticism and the feeling that you are "not enough" are destructive. Let's fully accept ourselves for who we are. We are all wonderful in our own unique ways. Enjoy!

I believe cultivating a strong, grounded, and healthy sense of self-love is one of the greatest gifts you can give to yourself because it is the foundation for abundance and love in your life. The standard you set for yourself is the standard by which you teach other people how to treat you. You are the measuring stick, and you set up the idea that others must strive to live up to if they want the privilege and honor of being a valued member of your life.

Building a firm sense of self-love takes a high level of time and commitment. Building self-love requires a lot of unlearning the stories of about yourself authored by other people instead of by you. Building self-love requires you to learn to see yourself clearly as you are with all your imperfections and all the wonderful gifts that you can give to the world.

Website: 11DreamsGoGetter.com

No person is all bad, nor all good. Healthy self-love requires that you put as much study into knowing your strengths as into knowing your weaknesses. It is really about developing awareness so you can see yourself through the lens of reality and not through a warped lens that accentuates your perceived shortcomings and turns them into a chronic habit of proclaiming all the ways you are not good enough. Self-love is about coming back home to who we originally entered the world as, so that we can tune into the amazing gift of our true self. We then, learn from that and, shine brightly as who we truly are and let that be our gift and legacy to the world. Self-love is a courageous act! We are bombarded with messages of what is lacking in us from the moment we come into the world until the moment we leave. Unfortunately, there are NOT many billboards or TV commercials that loudly state, "You are wonderful just as you are!" Our society benefits on us, feeling like we need to do more, have more, and be more in order to be worthy of love, success, or any of the feel-good things in life. But, that is simply not true.

Committing to self-love is a courageous and bold act. It is truly a revolutionary way to live your life because it is the willingness to create space for yourself so much so that your inner voice becomes louder than any external voice. It is the audacity to be happy as you are, with what you have got, and the humility to do what is within your power to change your situation and make it better. Not because a commercial ad told you that you will not be good enough until you lose 30lbs or because the latest TV show made you feel like you need to be in a relationship to be happy. It is about living from an internal center of control so that you are the director of the movie of your life and you are the star. You do things because they fill you up with joy and lift your spirits. Self-love frees you from keeping up with the Joneses...or the Kardashians.

Self-love allows you to create a life that is in line with your own internal value system and on your own timeline. Self-love allows you to open up to the possibility that life is happening FOR you not TO you and that the things you go through are helping you move into a space of self-compassion and acceptance. They help shape you and help you discover the source of the greatest gifts you own and can give because the pain of that event or the joy of that other event can only serve to help you better connect with others on a deeper level. We can only meet other people as deeply as we have met ourselves. If we do not create space to know ourselves intimately, sit with our own joy and sorrows, and exercise empathy, understanding, and honesty with ourselves first, how can we ever expect to give that beautiful gift to anyone else or be capable of receiving it.

Additionally, everything we do in life requires dealing with people in some way, shape, or form. For too long there has been too heavy an emphasis on developing IQ over EQ and "hard skills" over "soft skills." You can be the richest man/woman in the world and still have your heart broken. Knowing how to navigate through the pain and emotional discomfort is not something you are likely to learn in school. And, it is, unfortunately, something that too many people make it through their whole lives without learning! To do anything great or small requires some level of connection with other human beings. And again, if you have not truly learned how to connect with yourself, love yourself, hold space for yourself, cope and depend on yourself, then your capacity to do that for another human being will be so low. Often, I see relationships, whether they are friendships, professional, or romantic, crumble quickly at the first sign of conflict or discomfort because no one is willing to show up in honesty nor is there a collective capacity for deeper understanding and empathy. This is how we get a disposal rich culture where you simply swipe the person out of your life, and you are on to the next, ready to fall into the same patterns and get the same results.

It gets worse when relationships die an excruciating death, slowly eroding over time because no one is willing to show up, be present, and do whatever it takes to move the life of the relationship forward. Or perhaps it is simply because they would rather be together than face life on their own.

Most of the time, life seems so hard to face as an individual person because that person has not learned to see and accept that he/she is whole and complete on his/her own. He/she has not developed his/her self-love sufficiently and thus goes through the world looking to use other people as a crutch or plug or blinder to what is missing inside him/her.

Self-love with awareness is the antidote to this. Self-love permits you to do the work to fill spirit up so much so that you cannot exist in the world without overflowing with joy, love, sorrow, empathy, and all the other wonderfully raw and real natural parts of being a human being. Self-love awakens you to the fact that you were, are, and always will be a whole and a complete person no matter what stage of life experience you are in. It allows you to come home to yourself and have the capacity to sit with whatever guest shows up to visit your home, be it grief, loneliness, awkwardness, awe, joy, or contentment. Living with self-love as your baseline allows you to show up in the world not looking to others to get certain needs met but looking to yourself. It allows you to show up and focus on what value you can bring to the moment, and of course, it allows you to receive joy instead of neediness.

Self-love is a game changer when truly embraced. It revolutionizes your experiences, gives self-confidence to weather any storm, but ultimately allows for deeper love and connection with others because you have developed the capacity for deep love and connection with yourself first.

ABOUT THE AUTHOR

Sabrina He was born and raised in Shaoguan, China. Her formal name is Yan Chang He. She graduated with a bachelor degree in Biology Education in China and an MBA degree in America.

She has dared to dream big since high school. She devotes her life to follow her heart and pursue her dreams. She started her journey and adventures in June 2004 when she flew to the United States alone with a big red suitcase and a heart full of dreams. By the time this book was published, she actualized 6 of her dreams. She is determined not to stop taking actions until all her 11 dreams become a reality.

Her journey to her dreams has been a rollercoaster. It is full of ups and downs. It is filled with passion, fear, laughter, excitement, tears, struggles, doubt, sadness, hope, love, fulfillment, faith and self-discovery. She invites you to immerse into her life story and discover how to live your dreams through self-discipline.

As a single mom with a young child, she manages to get up at 3:00 a.m. every morning to exercise and work on her dreams. She shares her secret to self-discipline in this book to show you the path to living your dreams someday soon.

She wants to touch millions of people's lives by lighting up the path to living their dreams. To help her reach more people who want to be truly alive, she will be very grateful if you will post a short review if you enjoyed this book or found it useful. Together, we can make this world a better place where hearts are filled with joy, fulfillment and vibrant color.

This is the end of this book. I hope that my story has inspired you to pursue your dreams. If you are sick and tired of being stuck in life and you are ready to do whatever it takes to achieve the ultimate lifestyle that you desire, reach out to me at: 11DREAMSBOOK@GMAIL.COM
Hope to hear from you soon!!!

Bibliography

(n.d.). Retrieved from Good Reads: https://www.goodreads.com/quotes/144299-the-bad-news-is-time-flies-the-good-news-is

(1947, September). *The Reader's Digest, Volume 51*, p. 64.

(2015). Retrieved from I AM CHRISTIAN: http://christiansblogss.blogspot.com

Admin. (2009, May 12). *Everyone Sells*. Retrieved from Success.com: https://www.success.com/everyone-sells/

Agnihotri, N. (2019). *Procrasdemon - The Artist's Guide to Liberation From Procrastination.*

Angelou, M. (2011, July 4). *Angelou's Facebook*. Retrieved from Facebook: https://www.facebook.com/MayaAngelou/posts/10150251846629796

Autherine, J. (2018). *Wild Heart, Peaceful Soul: Poems and Inspiration to Live and Love Harmoniously.* Autherine Publishing.

Bleiler, G. (2010, December 10). Why Olympian Gretchen Bleiler is Unstoppable. (Cosmogirl, Interviewer) Retrieved from https://www.seventeen.com/life/a13074/gretchen-bleiler-interview/

Boehner, J. (2012, August 29). *John Boehner RNC speech (text and video)*. Retrieved from politico.com: https://www.politico.com/story/2012/08/john-boehner-rnc-speech-transcript-080377

Boiling frog. (2018, November). Retrieved from Wikipedia: https://en.wikipedia.org

Brown, H. J. (1990). *P.S. I Love You*. Nashville, Tennessee, United States: Rutledge Hill Press, a Thomas Nelson Company. Retrieved from https://quoteinvestigator.com/2011/09/29/you-did/#note-2779-4

Cardone, G. (2016). *Be Obsessed or Be Average*. New York: Penguin Random House LLC.

Cardone, G. (2016, September 25). *Grant Cardone*. Retrieved from Facebook.com: https://www.facebook.com/grantcardonefan/photos/a.1015010313 2168563/10154479087028563/?type=3&theater

Carnegie, D. (1984). *How to Stop Worrying and Start Living Revised Edition 1984*. (D. Carnegie, Ed.) New York: Simon & Schuster, Inc.

Carrey, J. (2014, May 24). *Jim Carrey Commencement Speech*. Retrieved from Maharishi University of Management: https://www.mum.edu/whats-happening/graduation-2014/full-jim-carrey-address-video-and-transcript/

Coelho, P. (2008). *The Winner Stands Alone, Original title: O Vencedor está Só*. (M. J. Costa, Trans.) Portuguese, Brazil: HarperCollins.

Coupland, D. (1993). *Shampoo Planet*. Washington Square Press.

Dean, Z. (2013, June 27). *Not everyone will understand your journey*. Retrieved from Blog Zero Dean: https://web.archive.org/web/20130805053030/http://blog.zerodean.com/2013/tao-of-zero/not-everyone-will-understand-your-journey

Dean, Z. (2018). *Lessons Learned from The Path Less Traveled*.

Disraeli, B. (1844). *Coningsby; Or, The New Generation*. London: Henry Colburn Publisher.

Eliot, T. S. (1931). *Preface to "Transit of Venus" (Poems by Harry Crosby)*. Paris: Black Sun Press.

Faudet, M. (2017). *Smoke & Mirrors*. Andrews McMeel Publishing.

Fitzgerald, T. (1980s). Retrieved from http://marciodisneyarchives.blogspot.com/2011/07/if-we-can-dream-it-we-can-do-it.html

Foer, J. S. (2005). *Extremely Loud and Incredibly Close*. Mariner Books.

Gazipura, A. (2017). *Not Nice*. Portland: B C Allen Publishing And Tonic Books.

Hale, M. (2013). *The Single Woman: Life, Love, and a Dash of Sass.* Thomas Nelson.

Henley, W. E. (1888). *Book of Verses.* England: Book of Verses.

Hill, N. (1937). *Think and Grow Rich.* Napoleon Hill Foundation.

Ingersoll, R. G. (1876, July 4). Independence Day speech. Peoria, Illinois. Retrieved from https://www.askideas.com/the-greatest-test-of-courage-on-earth-is-to-bear-defeat-without-losing-heart/

Jobs, S. (2005, June 14). *'You've got to find what you love,' Jobs says.* Retrieved from Stanford News: https://news.stanford.edu/2005/06/14/jobs-061505/

JOHNSON, Z. (2014, Febury 27). *Leah Remini Reveals She Left Scientology for Her Daughter Sofia.* Retrieved from Enews: https://www.eonline.com/news/515365/leah-remini-reveals-she-left-scientology-for-her-daughter-sofia

Larche, J. (2016). *Five Loaves, Two Fish: Your Little is Never Too Small In The Hands of a Big God.* CreateSpace Independent Publishing Platform.

LEONARD, L. (1987, March 17). *Former President Richard Nixon said Tuesday a fearless attitude...* Retrieved from UPI.COM: https://www.upi.com/Archives/1987/03/17/Former-President-Richard-Nixon-said-Tuesday-a-fearless-attitude/4779542955600/

Lincicome, B. (1977, April 14). Fort Lauderdale News. *Ali, Louis: The Spectre of Greatness Past (Continuation title: More Lincicome),* Start Page 1D, Quote Page 6D, Column 1. Retrieved from Newspapers_com; https://quoteinvestigator.com/category/muhammad-ali/#note-435796-1

Maraboli, S. (2009). *Life, the Truth, and Being Free.* Better Today Publishing.

Maya Angelou: In her own words. (2014, May 28). Retrieved from BBC News: https://www.bbc.com/news/world-us-canada-27610770

McClone, M. (2013). *Mistletoe Magic* (Vols. Bar V5 Dude Ranch #2, Copper Mountain Christmas #3). Tule Publishing Group.

McGraw, T., & Douglas., T. (2006). My Little Girl [Recorded by T. McGraw]. [Song].

McWilliams, P. (1994). *Do It!: Let's Get Off Our Buts.* Prelude Press.

Milton, J. (1667). *Paradise Lost, Book 1*. London: Samuel Simmons (original).

Minkoff, R. (Director). (2003). *The Haunted Mansion* [Motion Picture].

Mirow, D. (1986, March 30). Cleveland Plain Dealer. *Fighting for kids is a full-time job*, Page 21, Column 2 thru 4. Retrieved from https://quoteinvestigator.com/2019/04/18/staircase/#note-135686-1

Muhammad Ali: In His Own Words. (2016, June 5). Retrieved from CBS News: https://www.cbsnews.com/news/muhammad-ali-in-his-own-words/

Pavlina, S. (2008). *Personal Development for Smart People*. Los Vegas: HAY House, Incorporated.

Pickle, B. (1981, October 11). Sentinel Al-Anon Helps Family, Friends to Orderly Lives. *The Knoxville News*, F17, Column 2. Retrieved from https://quoteinvestigator.com/2017/03/23/same/#note-15768-2

Qualls, T. L. (2019). *Painted Oxen*. Homebound Publications.

Quinn, D. (1996). *The Story of B*. Bantam Publishing.

Rohn, J. (2013, February 24). *Jim Rohn*. Retrieved from FaceBook.com: https://www.facebook.com/OfficialJimRohn/posts/time-is-more-valuable-than-money-you-can-get-more-money-but-you-cannot-get-more-/10152568862235635/

Rohn, J. (2017, August 29). *Jim Rohn*. Retrieved from FaceBook.com: https://www.facebook.com/OfficialJimRohn/posts/if-you-work-on-your-job-youll-make-a-living-if-you-work-on-yourself-youll-make-a/10159226981300635/

Rohn, J. (2017, February 15). *The Key to Getting All You Want? Discipline*. Retrieved from jimrohn.com: https://www.jimrohn.com/?s=For+every+disciplined+effort%2C+there+are+multiple+rewards

Rohn, J. (2018, October 15). *Being Successful Is a Personal Choice*. Retrieved from jimrohn.com: https://www.jimrohn.com/success-is-a-personal-choice/

Schuller, R. H. (1984). *Tough Times Never Last, But Tough People Do!* Bantam.

Sherman, J. R. (1982). *Rejection*. Golden Valley, Minnesota, U.S.A.: Pathway Books.

Solomon, D. (2010, March 4). *The Priest.* Retrieved from The New York Times Magazine: https://www.nytimes.com/2010/03/07/magazine/07fob-q4-t.html

Strode, M. (1903, August). Wind-Wafted Wild Flowers. *The Open Court: Devoted to the Science of Religion, the Religion of Science, and the Extension of the Religious Parliament Idea, 17, Number 8, Section: Miscellaneous*, pp. Start Page 505, Quote Page 505. Retrieved from https://quoteinvestigator.com/2014/06/19/new-path/#note-9179-2

Swindoll, C. R. (2006). *The Grace Awakening.* Thomas Nelson.

The Water in You: Water and the Human Body. (2019). Retrieved from Science For A Changing World: https://www.usgs.gov

Tracy, B. (2014, April 20). *Tracy, Brian.* Retrieved from FaceBook: http://www.facebook.com

Twain, M. (1904). *Notebook.*

What Oprah Knows for Sure About Life's Biggest Adventure. (2002, July). *O, The Oprah Magazine.* Retrieved from Oprah.com: http://www.oprah.com/spirit/what-oprah-knows-for-sure-about-lifes-biggest-adventure

Williams, P. (2004). *How to Be Like Walt: Capturing the Magic Every Day of Your Life.* Health Communications Inc.

Winfrey, O. (2012, April 2). *Oprah Winfrey.* Retrieved from FaceBook.com: https://www.facebook.com/oprahwinfrey/posts/courage-is-feeling-the-fear-and-doing-it-anyway/221105204663913/

World Birth & Death Rates. (2011). Retrieved from Ecology Global Network: https://Ecology.com

Zuck, R. B. (2009). *The Speaker's Quote Book: Over 5,000 Illustrations and Quotations for All Occasions.* Kregel Academic & Professional. Retrieved from https://quotes.yourdictionary.com/author/quote/574189

www.ingramcontent.com/pod-product-compliance
Lightning Source LLC
Chambersburg PA
CBHW052012090426

42741CB00008B/1656